DID JESUS WRITE THIS BOOK?

A Study of THE BOOK OF THE SECRETS OF ENOCH

Reappraising it in the light of the Qumran, Chenoboskion, and other recently discovered manuscripts and papyri

With a rendering into modern English, based on a conflation of many texts and versions.

Did Jesus
Write This Book?

Charles Francis Potter

A FAWCETT CREST BOOK

FAWCETT PUBLICATIONS, INC., GREENWICH, CONN.
MEMBER OF AMERICAN BOOK PUBLISHERS COUNCIL, INC.

"And there are also many other things which Jesus did, the which, if they should be written every one, I suppose that even the world itself could not contain the books that should be written" (John 21:25)

Contents

CHAPTER 1

Haunted by an Idea

For years I had been peculiarly attracted—even fascinated—by a strange book discovered in Serbia by English scholars in 1892 but translated from a text first written in the days when Jesus was on earth. The book was variously named by the few authorities who have studied it as the Book of the Secrets of Enoch, or as Slavonic Enoch (from the language of the copies found), or Second Enoch (because it has been dated as later than the better-known Ethiopic or First Enoch).

Behind the ancient literary mask of Enoch—"the seventh from Adam," as Jude designates him (verse 14 in his Epistle)—there are a number of prophetic minds of the centuries between the Old and New Testaments. Four different Enochs are mentioned in the Book of Genesis, but the one with whom we deal is the son of Jared, who "walked with God and was not; for God took him" (Genesis 5:18 and 24), which is interpreted to mean that the son of Jared, like Elijah, never saw death.

The great importance of his name as a contributor to

early Christian literature is based on the references to his writings by the Church Fathers. One of the most eminent of them, Augustine, is reported as saying that the Church excluded the First Enoch from the canon of the New Testament only because it purported to go back to primeval times, even before the creation of the world!

Nevertheless, Enoch's revelations were more favored by the early Christians than by the orthodox rabbis and their congregations who disapproved of his omniscience. Whatever the reason, it is surmised that First Enoch was deliberately "lost" for some fifteen centuries until it turned up in Abyssinia in the eighteenth century, translated into Ethiopian. Similarly, The Secrets of Enoch was "lost" for some twelve hundred years before it turned up in Serbia in the nineteenth century, translated into Slavonic. Both translations were at hand to be checked with the Dead Sea Scrolls that came to light in the twentieth century.

Make of these remarkable facts what you will!

When I first came upon the Book of the Secrets of Enoch while a student in the theological seminary, I read and reread the 1896 English translation by Canon R. H. Charles and Dr. W. R. Morfill. My mind became saturated with its quaint phraseology and impressive ideas. More than charmed, I was completely captivated.

In due course, when I went on to study other non-biblical Jewish literature of the period between Malachi and Matthew, such as the Book of Jubilees, First Enoch, the Testaments of the Twelve Patriarchs and the Psalms of Solomon, with the idea of a doctoral thesis proving their influence on Christian origins, and particularly on the New Testament, I also naturally culled from The Secrets of Enoch.

Interesting, and often pertinent, as the other intertestamental books were, The Secrets seemed to me to possess a *something* that the others lacked. There was a quality about it—a certain mystic radiance—that attracted me yet eluded my grasp. Whenever I thought of it, which was often, I felt the glow one feels when recalling a precious secret memory which is his own intimate possession. And there was an aura of "rosemary for remembrance" about it, which seemed to evoke the echo of monastery chimes heard long ago.

This endured for some time—a pleasant awareness of something beautiful, a group of related thoughts and fancies which I could call up and ponder during rare moments of leisure in busy pastorates. Indeed, I suppose the Enochan literature eventually became my private area of retreat from the mad whirl of forty clerical years in New York City.

But in my subconscious a seed had germinated and a new concept was evolving. The more I studied the book and meditated upon it, the more impressed I became by the peculiar similarity of its phrases and thought-forms to those of Jesus, as quoted in the Gospels. Throughout the book are repeated his favorite teachings about charity, forgiveness, love of neighbor and the endurance of affliction, as well as his warnings about Kingdom Come, hell, punishment and his promises of eternal life in heaven with him and the angels.

I checked these various similarities and parallels by noting in the margins of my copy of The Secrets of Enoch those Bible verses which the Enochan passages most closely resembled. I was surprised at the number of such similarities to verses in the four Gospels, in Paul's letters, in the anonymous Epistle to the Hebrews, and in the short works of James, Peter, John and Jude. But especially striking were the similarities to verses in the last book of the Christian Bible, which Protestants call "Revelation" and Roman Catholics call the "Apocalypse" (the Greek word for *revelation*). A book that is apocalyptic, such as Revelation or The Secrets of Enoch, supposedly reveals carefully concealed secrets.

This last book of the New Testament is entitled The Revelation of St. John the Divine, but the first verse states that it is "The Revelation of Jesus Christ," given to Jesus by God and relayed to John by an angel (thus paralleling God's revelation to Enoch, who, accompanied by angels, brought the "secrets" to earth).

Much of the Apocalypse purports to be the words of Jesus, as transmitted to John on Patmos by an angel (the passages are printed in red in the red-letter New Testaments, just as are the sayings of Jesus in the Gospels). But the entire last book of the New Testament is so full of quotations from, parallels with, and reminiscences of The Secrets of Enoch that if a Christian preacher announced he would read a passage of Revelation and then proceeded to read sections of The Secrets of Enoch, there would be very few, if any, in the congregation who would know the difference. In fact, some might like it better, for many early Christians preferred other apocalyptic books, including Enoch, to that of John, and only gave them up when Revelation, after a long controversy, was chosen as the last book of the official canon of the Bible.

But as I traced the various parallels between the intertestamental books and the New Testament, I continued to make marginal notes on my copy of The Secrets of Enoch. The germinating idea of the supreme importance of The Secrets of Enoch was still hidden in my subconscious, yet the satisfaction I derived from making these notations was out of all proportion to their real use in a task of average scholarly research.

Naturally, I also hunted tirelessly for every scrap of information about the book, but there were very few to be had. It had been known to western scholars only since 1892, and few commentaries were available for critical study. Those who had made a special study of this ancient and important book—and they could be counted on the fingers of one hand—agreed that it obviously had had considerable influence on the early Christian Church and its literature, that it had certainly been written between 30 B.C. and A.D. 70 (probably between A.D. 1 and 50), and that the author was unknown.

Then, one evening, as I was enjoying my study of the book, what had been an obscure subconscious idea suddenly burst into a flash of illumination: It occurred to me that perhaps *Jesus himself had written this book!*

I was staggered mentally. The sheer possibility of there being in existence, hitherto unrecognized, translated copies of a book actually composed and written by Jesus himself was altogether beyond reason or belief.

As soon as I had recovered a measure of composure, I asked myself, Why didn't I think of it before? And then I realized that I had been dimly aware of it for some time—that the idea had been hovering—baffling, vague—on the fringe of my consciousness, eluding my grasp; but now it shone with a brilliant clarity.

Again I thought, Why hasn't someone else seen this possibility? There were the coincidences and resemblances, often word for word, view for view, opinion for opinion, beatitude for beatitude—all plain enough now. Why had scholars failed to sense this stupendous possibility?

Imagine if my sudden flash of insight were true! For nineteen centuries Christendom has vainly wished it had something Jesus had written—something from his own pen. But all we have are second- or thirdhand—or perhaps even seventhhand—quotations from his teachings, as given in the New Testament and in the writings of the Church Fathers. Much excitement was stirred in theological circles by the finding, in 1946, of certain alleged sayings of Jesus in codices (bound manuscripts) in a grave at Chenoboskion in Upper Egypt. These are either Logia, alleged sayings of Jesus in collections supposedly used by early preachers, or Agrapha, sayings ascribed to him in Christian oral tradition or in post-biblical writings by the Church Fathers.

But these Logia and Agrapha, however valuable, do not rank as high as the canonical Gospels which claim to quote Jesus (although they frequently contradict each other, or vary greatly in their recording of the same quotation). Far more important than sayings, Gospels, traditions or the writing of Church Fathers would be a book —or even a page or two—composed by the one who called himself the Son of Man. *A single paragraph known to have been written by him would be beyond price!*

No, I tried to tell myself sensibly, it just can't be, and I did my best to dismiss the preposterous notion. But it kept thrusting itself on my attention. My mind remained under the spell of the ancient book. Somehow, the personality of Jesus seemed to glow through the pages—in some places, faintly, as in certain Bible passages; in others, as brightly as in the Sermon on the Mount, so similar in many verses to Enoch's beatitudes and his parting advice to his sons. From so much of The Secrets of Enoch did the radiance of Jesus emanate that I found it impossible to dismiss the thought that he might have written it.

So, to dispose of the idea properly, I recalled my college training in logic, argumentation, and debate and began to marshal arguments to prove that Jesus could not possibly have written such a book. Yet, as I went over the text and reviewed what scholars have deduced and inferred from both literary and historical criticism since the book came to light in 1892, I was amazed to find that there appeared to be no convincing evidence against Jesus' authorship. There were, to be sure, theories as to the nationality of the author and his probable background, but these theories did not necessarily exclude Jesus. So as I carefully and patiently sought reasons why he could not have written the book, I discovered more reasons to support my sudden idea that he might have.

For many months I debated the matter with myself, checking and rechecking all the evidence, pro and con. Naturally, I was hesitant about making a public announcement of such a momentous possibility until I could assemble stronger evidence. But the compelling conviction grew upon me that although Jesus might not have written every sentence or section of The Secrets of Enoch in its present form (for it must have gone through many hands), he was as much its author as Luke is the author of the Acts of the Apostles.

Yes, I concluded, here is a composition created during the lifetime of the Nazarene (but before any of the Gospels were written), a book whose authorship has not yet been determined, a book which contains many of the typical and distinctive ideas supposedly originated by Jesus and often expressed in his very words and phrases.

By 1924, after serious meditation and soul-searching, I felt not only justified in raising publicly the question of Jesus' possible authorship, but obligated to do so.

But when I had prepared an outline and sample chapters of a book setting forth my discovery, I found publishers very cool to the idea. It seemed that the word *apocrypha*, which was then loosely applied to any nonbiblical scripture, was associated in the public mind with something false, spurious, untrustworthy. (Its original and correct meaning, of course, is *hidden* or *secret*. An apocryphal book was a sort of sacred riddle, its solution hidden from all except the initiate to whom a revelation of the concealed meaning had been or soon would be made.) So publishers were very wary about any unorthodox religious book and doubly cautious about a book admittedly noncanonical and apocryphal. Five firms turned down my proposed book, and the only publisher who showed any real interest went bankrupt before the book was even half finished.

So I put the idea and the research material on the shelf. But I could not entirely forget the idea, and occasionally I took down the material to add to it or to mull over it fondly. Meanwhile I kept up with the new studies in noncanonical fields.

Now, however, nearly forty years later, the interest in both Bible study and in the publishing of unusual religious books has decidedly increased. The discovery and translation of the hundreds of Qumran cave manuscripts (improperly but now permanently named the "Dead Sea Scrolls") have revealed many more fragments of the apocryphal intertestamental books, with a great deal more nonbiblical material showing up among them than official canonical books of the Old Testament. Moreover, to the great chagrin of the orthodox, scholars are increasingly inclined to connect Jesus with the Qumran community of Essene Jews, either directly or through John the Baptist.

And, most important, since The Secrets of Enoch obviously parallels and closely resembles both this newfound literature of Qumran and the Gospel sayings and teachings of Jesus, the possibility—and even the probability—of Jesus having been the author of at least part of The Secrets of Enoch has become more apparent. Several more and better manuscripts of The Secrets of Enoch have come to light, apparently unnoticed by the scholars so busily occupied in defending orthodox Christianity from the dangerous Qumran and Chenoboskion manuscripts, which have resurrected the long-buried heresies of Enochan Essenism and Alexandrian Gnosticism. At any rate, whether or not Jesus was the author, the book was written during his lifetime by someone sympathetic with his ideas, and was accepted as Scripture by the early Christian Church. If Jesus was not the author, he quoted from it passages which have always been considered original with him. And if it can be proved that Jesus was the author of even a part of this very unusual book, that part should certainly be included in a place of special honor in the New Testament itself.

In beginning the discussion of the question of Jesus' authorship of the book, I propose (after giving a necessary chapter to the other literary productions of the period between the last books of the Old Testament and the first books of the New) to set down, first, the evidence as I see it; the parallels in language and teachings, and other corroborative and confirmatory evidence. Then, in succeeding chapters, I shall present the possible objections to Jesus' authorship and my answers to them.

This plan will afford at least an introduction to this complex but vital question. It may be that some scholar will come forward and demonstrate the impossibility of my theory, or that some authoritative manuscript may be discovered. But it also may well be that someone will provide additional facts to support my theory—perhaps, again, from among Qumran cave fragments yet to be discovered and deciphered. Such facts, as yet unknown, may prove beyond doubt or cavil that we do have in The

Secrets of Enoch an authentic Scripture from the very hand of Jesus.

Whatever conclusion is reached, two desirable ends will be attained by patience and open-minded discussion. Inevitably, public interest will be stimulated in the neglected intertestamental writings in general and in The Secrets of Enoch in particular. These works deserve the attention of all Christians, for a knowledge of them is absolutely necessary to a better understanding of the New Testament, and would correct a number of mistaken interpretations on which whole denominations are based! Few Christians, especially in the United States, have ever heard of these books, for many of them were not included in the fourteen books of the official Apocrypha, which has been excluded of late from even the fine-print intertestamental limbo in Protestant Bibles, although retained in the Roman Catholic Scriptures. And as for Christian clergymen and priests, those who have read any appreciable amount of the Enochan and related apocalyptic literature are few, and those aware of its historic significance are even fewer.

The second desirable result to be expected from this proposed discussion will be the creation of sufficient interest in The Secrets of Enoch to cause a complete search to be made for more manuscripts of the text, not only in countries where other Slavonic copies might be brought to light, but also in Syria, Armenia, Egypt and particularly in Ethiopia, where James Bruce found the three manuscripts of the long-lost First Enoch. Apocryphal scriptures exist in Greek, Latin, Slavonic, Ethiopic, Coptic, Syriac, Hebrew, Aramaic, Arabic and Armenian, and it is probable that The Secrets of Enoch was translated into one or more of these languages. Since the Koran contains echoes and even a verbatim quotation from the book, it is possible that an Arabic text lies hidden in some ancient mosque. Or a Greek or Syriac version may still exist in a remote monastery or hermit scholar's library, unknown save to two or three local priests or monks. A fragment of it may have been copied in a parchment or papyrus codex with some other book. (Parts of unrelated books were sometimes copied on unused portions or blank pages of old manuscripts, and the several treatises in the roll or codex were then listed or cataloged under the name of the first or longest composition.)

Or part of the book may yet be found in palimpsest form. When parchment was scarce or expensive (and when were scholars not poor?), it was the custom of frugal authors and copyists to take an old manuscript of little current interest, scrape or otherwise erase the original writing, and then use the space for their own compositions. Since it is often possible to restore the original text by careful chemical or ray treatment, The Secrets of Enoch may yet be found, hidden under a later work. I have been told that there are in Istanbul and Antioch whole rooms full of ancient manuscripts not yet properly cataloged.

There is a lamentable lack of exchange of information among erudite scholars in different parts of the world, especially between those of different religions, or different sects of the same religion.

There should be available to every scholar a complete list of the contents of every manuscript, codex or book of Christian Scripture—apocryphal or not—and of the earlier commentaries on them. Until that monumental list is compiled, we cannot say whether or not there are in existence other manuscripts of The Secrets of Enoch. Secrecy, jealousy, provincialism and even downright ignorance have kept scholars of one country from knowing of the existence, much less the contents, of important manuscripts in other countries.

For instance, the late Dr. R. H. Charles, the great English authority on intertestamental scriptures, discovered the existence of The Secrets of Enoch only in 1892, but Russian scholars had long known of it, and had published it in Slavonic in Moscow in 1880. Dr. Charles' English translations, published in 1896 and 1912, are still not known except to a few theological seminary professors. Yet the book is of undeniable importance to every Christian and should be available to all Sunday School teachers, for it provides an insight into the thoughts of Jesus, and the Dead Sea Scrolls emphasize the importance of such knowledge.

CHAPTER 2

Scriptures Not in the Bible

Three fourths of the way through the Protestant Bible, the reader finds a break in the text where the Old Testament ends and the New Testament begins—or, to put it another way, where the Jewish Bible ends and the Christian additions begin. When he finishes the Book of Malachi, the reader is confronted with a blank page which he must turn before he can read the Gospel which bears the name of Saint Matthew. This is the only blank page in the Christian Bible. And it is sadly symbolic, for it marks the division between Jew and Christian—a division which need not have occurred and which may yet be healed, provided the scriptures which once bridged that yawning gap can be restored.

The New Testament is often printed in red-letter editions in which the words attributed to Jesus are printed in red ink to contrast with the black ink of the rest of the text. The red color is supposed to recall the blood of Jesus "shed on Calvary to atone for the sins of the world." Perhaps the blank page that divides the testaments should also be a deep crimson to symbolize the seas of blood shed by poor persecuted peoples in the religious quarrels between the two faiths over the centuries. If only understanding and friendship had prevailed over ignorance and fanaticism!

The average Christian layman today (and many a clergyman) is unaware of the sad fact that in turning that blank but eloquent page he is omitting several centuries of important and inspiring literature. Whole books belong there—books once regarded by both Jews and Christians (and by heretics and Muslims, too) as sacred.

These intertestamental books were scriptures which Jesus and his disciples loved and quoted with approval and appreciation. In a sense, one might well say that these books were in Jesus' Bible. They are not in ours— largely because of the suspicion, jealousy, bitterness, and hatred of earlier centuries.

It was the custom, as late as the nineteenth century, to include a few of the less representative of these books in the Protestant Bible, but with rigid reservations. Old family Bibles of the King James Version sometimes contained a section between Malachi and Matthew—the Apocrypha, which consisted of fourteen books, from First Esdras to Second Maccabees. The text was printed in small type to indicate that these books were not considered on a par with the rest of the Bible. For many years now, however, the Bibles in circulation among Protestant Christians have left out the Apocrypha altogether. Roman Catholic Bibles, on the other hand, still include a dozen books of the Apocrypha, inserted at various places throughout the Old Testament.

The Protestant Apocrypha included only a few of the many interesting books written in the intertestamental period. Many of the most valuable compositions of that time—books which had a great influence on the thought of Jesus and his contemporaries—are to be found neither in the Old Testament nor in the Apocrypha. They were excluded by the Jews before A.D. 100, and by Christians as the canonical Bible gradually took shape and was compiled about A.D. 400. Then they soon dropped out of sight (their disappearance frequently assisted by the more orthodox Church Fathers) and for centuries were lost to Christendom.

Many manuscripts and fragments of the excluded books have recently come to light from the Qumran caves by the Dead Sea and the Chenoboskion cave in Upper Egypt. The Qumran find is dated by scholars as the spring of 1947 (although the Bedouin boy who found the first cave now says it was 1945), while the Chenoboskion discovery took place in 1946, or possibly in 1945. The extent and significance of both finds have so far been only partially and very tardily revealed, but the heretics, both Jewish and Christian, are having their side presented at last.

Most scholars now call this collection of excluded books the "pseudepigrapha" (pronounced *soo-de-*PIG-*rah-fah*), from the Greek *pseud* (meaning *false*, in the sense of *pretended* or *assumed*) and *epigraph* (meaning *signature*). The books in the group were given this name because most of them bear the name of some famous Old Testament patriarch, such as Abraham, Moses, Enoch or Solomon. In reality, of course, they were composed many centuries after their deaths.

The custom of attributing a book to a revered patriarch was not uncommon in those troubled days, and its purpose was not merely to add prestige to the work, it was far more important as a device for keeping the true author anonymous because, according to the Old Testament Book of the Prophecies of Zechariah (13:3), anyone who presumed to "prophesy" after the time of Ezra (when the Torah was supposed to have been completed) was subject to the death penalty, which was to be inflicted by his own parents.

The custom persists: Modern writers sometimes find it advisable to use pseudonyms or pen names, especially if what they have to say is unconventional or too progressive, as were the contents of these pseudepigraphic books.

The name pseudepigrapha is unsatisfactory, however, because some of the books in the collection—the Book of Jubilees, for instance (often called "Little Genesis" because it fills in the gaps of "Big Genesis," even telling where Cain got his wife)—have no signature at all. On the other hand, there are several "falsely signed" books in the Old Testament, such as the Book of Daniel, which contains the statement: "In the third year of the reign of King Belshazzar, a vision appeared unto me, even unto me, Daniel. . . ." Evidence in the Book of Daniel itself indicates that it was written long after Belshazzar and the other Babylonians were conquered by the Persians and the Persians, in turn, were conquered by the Greeks.

Unsatisfactory and inaccurate as the word pseudepigrapha may be, it must be used, for it has been generally accepted by scholars to designate a special group of books, most of them written between 200 B.C. and A.D. 100, which are not included in our Bible nor in its Apocrypha, when it had one.

Some Roman Catholic scholars, however, refer to the pseudepigrapha as part of the general classification of apocrypha. It seems not yet to be generally known in America, nor by Protestants anywhere, that the Catholics stole a march on their Christian brethren several years ago by publishing *La Bible Apocryphe*, containing the usual pseudepigraphic books, Ethiopic Enoch, Slavonic Enoch, the Book of Jubilees, the Testaments of the Twelve Patriarchs, the Psalms of Solomon, the Sibylline Oracles, the Letters of Aristeas, the Life of Adam and Eve, the Assumption of Moses, the Ascension of Isaiah, Fourth Maccabees, Fourth Ezra and Second and Third Baruch.

The significant thing about this collection of apocrypha, published in Paris in 1953 with official imprimatur, with a splendid introduction (scholarly, but safely orthodox) by Daniel-Rops and with the texts chosen and translated by the brilliant Professor Bonsirven of L'Institut Biblique Pontifical of Rome, is that it also includes, under the rather ambiguous title *La Nouvelle Alliance de Damas*, all the new books from the Qumran Dead Sea caves which had been identified up to that time!

So, in a sort of literary baptism, Daniel-Rops and Bonsirven, with the blessing of Rome, have included in *La Bible Apocryphe*, right between the Psalms of Solomon and the Sibylline Oracles, the Qumran finds: namely, the Zadokite or Damascus Document, the *pesher* or commentary on Habakkuk, the Rule of the Community (known to Protestants as the Manual of Discipline), Parts I and II, the War of the Sons of Light Against the Sons of Darkness and a selection of the Hymns or Psalms of Thanksgiving.

Not one Christian in ten thousand, however, Catholic or Protestant, has read or even seen the Books of Enoch, the Book of Jubilees, the Psalms of Solomon (quoted by Jesus in Gethsemane: "My soul is exceeding sorrowful into death" [Mark:14-34]) or the Testaments of the Twelve Patriarchs (quoted in the Sermon on the Mount). They are studied only by a few scholarly clergymen and small groups of professors and students in theological seminaries. They are as inaccessible to the general public as the whole Bible was in the early Middle Ages. Yet these practically unknown compositions had more influence on the writers of the New Testament than did the books of the Old Testament. Informed scholars regard a knowledge of the pseudepigrapha as indispensable and essential to an understanding of the New Testament and Christianity itself.

To the average Sunday School teacher or confirmed Bible reader, the blank page between Malachi and Matthew represents a period when no prophet spoke and no spiritual psalms were written or sung, a Dark Ages during which the light of truth failed. Many a sermon eloquently depicts the advent of Jesus as the sudden dawning of the Sun of Righteousness, shining all the more brightly because of the hopeless blackness of the period which preceded his coming.

Nothing could be farther from the truth. Dr. R. H. Charles, in *Religious Development Between the Old and*

New Testaments, points out that the two centuries preceding the birth of Christ were "far from being ages of spiritual stagnation and darkness"; they were really "the two most fruitful centuries in religious life and thought in the history of Israel."

To put it in modern terms, we might say that the pseudepigraphic books were the popular "bestsellers" of a period of revived interest in religion, a time during which Hillel, Gamaliel, Philo, Simon Magus, Josephus, John the Baptist, Jesus and Paul were among the inspired thinkers, teachers, writers and prophets. The orthodox religionists of the day looked down upon the new prophets and bitterly criticized those who had added to the old religion the new emphasis of apocalypse and Kingdom Come, just as some of the orthodox religious spokesmen of today are criticizing the new prophets, preachers and writers who are adding to the old religion the new emphases of psychology and psychiatry.

It was that religious belief and thought of the pseudepigraphic writings which nourished the mind and spirit of Jesus. Undoubtedly, he read widely and deeply in the rich apocalyptic and philosophic literature produced in his lifetime and during the two centuries before his birth. Prophecy and poetry, apocalypse and psalm, proverb and wisdom, history and biography, fable, myth and parable—all these he found in the pseudepigrapha, and it is now evident that he read them thoroughly and often until he made this precious heritage his own.

He also read the books we call the Old Testament. He liked the Prophets and the Psalms, and the Book of Deuteronomy. (It is noteworthy, in this connection, that his favorites—Deuteronomy, Isaiah and the Psalms—were also the favorites of the Qumran community, whose unearthed library contains many copies of those books.) But, like any good Jew, although he paid due deference to the Torah, especially as given in Deuteronomy, he did not hesitate to take issue with it on some points or even to suggest amendments to it. He was in constant conflict with the Pharisees, who insisted on the observance of the Law in its minutest points. By the same token, he may also have differed with the members of the Qumran community, who were even more meticulous in their adherence to the Law. That may be why he apparently left the hard legalists of that community later and went out and formed his own splinter group of Reformed Essenes, as John the Baptist seems to have done at about the same time.

Jesus was nonetheless a good Jew when he argued with Pharisee or Essene against their strict legalism; he was simply representing the new reform spirit in Judaism against the old, conservative stand-patters of Israel. And that new spirit of progressive Judaism already had its own literature, which he apparently regarded as no less sacred than the older Law and the Prophets.

He was familiar, of course, with the older Jewish literature. He adapted and used for his message the parts he liked; but the newer Jewish literature attracted him more. He took for his own its radical new doctrines, such as those of the Son of Man, the New Jerusalem, the Second Coming, the Millennium and Judgment Day. These apocalyptic ideas were not acceptable to the more conservative Jews and inevitably brought Jesus into conflict with them. The conflict led to his death, but did not end with it.

A true understanding of Jesus requires a knowledge of the literature that gave him his inspiration and much of his message. A knowledge of the Old Testament cannot adequately explain Jesus and early Christianity; so old-time theologians had to postulate a miracle. The New Testament assumes new dimensions after one reads and ponders the books Jesus read and pondered. The Old Testament has bulked larger in the thought of the Christian Church than it did in the thought of Jesus, while these pseudepigraphic books which he admired have been strangely neglected.

Jesus respected the Old Testament, but he must have loved these other writings. He quoted and took texts from them for his sermons. Their very phrases became part of his vocabulary, and their doctrines—many of which are not found in the Old Testament—were the ones he constantly preached and taught.

Many of the sayings which have been thought original with him are quotations from the pseudepigrapha. And one pseudepigraph contains so many of his words and ideas that it may well be that he wrote it, or part of it.

CHAPTER 3

Some Striking Parallels

Many of the words and phrases in this anonymous
Secrets of Enoch are remarkably like the ones Jesus used,
as recorded in the four Gospels of the New Testament.
Even whole sentences from the book appear in his parables, beatitudes and discussions.

For instance, the author of the Gospel "according to
John" reports at length Jesus' conversation with his disciples at the Last Supper. In answering a question by
Simon Peter during that simple and very solemn meal,
Jesus made a memorable promise concerning a future life
—a promise which has been the source of infinite consolation to generations of Christians. At almost all fu-
neral or memorial services—whatever the denomination
—the precious words are repeated for the comfort of
mourners.

Jesus, seated at the table, had said he was going away,
and Peter naturally asked where he was going. In his
rather indirect answer, Jesus said, "In my Father's house

are many mansions: if it were not so, I would have told you. I go to prepare a place for you" (John 14:2).

The beautiful chapter 61 of The Secrets of Enoch records Enoch's farewell talk at his last meal with his children, his household and "the elders of the people." Before the two angels escorted him "to the highest heaven, where the Lord welcomed him and gave him a place in His Presence forever" (67:2), Enoch said:

> "Now then, my children, keep your hearts from all untruth, which the Lord hates, but, much more, abstain from any prejudice against any living soul which the Lord has created. That which a man asks from the Lord for his own soul, let him pray that He do it likewise for every living soul. For in the Great Age to come, as I well know, many mansions are prepared for men, very good dwellings (for the good), and bad ones without number (for the bad). Blessed are those who shall move into the good mansions, for in the bad ones there is [no rest and] no repentance" (61:1-3).

This passage answers a question raised by the King James Bible version of John's Gospel: How can there be many mansions in a house? It becomes clear that John must have condensed the statement; Jesus probably said, in effect: "Heaven is where my Father lives. In the future time when you go there you will find many mansions, and I am going there ahead of you to prepare a good place for you."

Recent translators of this verse use the phrase "many rooms" rather than "many mansions," but that does violence to the Greek text and rather belittles heaven. The Greek words seem to convey the idea, well expressed in The Secrets of Enoch, of a large settlement—a colony or community of many dwellings.

Another question is raised by the King James phrasing of the rather peculiar sentence, "If it were not so, I would have told you," which strikes one as somewhat abrupt and gratuitous. No improvement is the version offered by certain recent translators: "If it were not so, would I have told you that I go to prepare a place for you?" Jesus had not so far told them that, anyway, and the remark seems superfluous and out of context.

But that sort of remark, implying knowledge of such secret matters as the dwelling arrangements in heaven and the preparations there for the future participants in the Messianic Feast, is common enough in The Secrets of Enoch; in fact, it is one frequently made by Enoch to assure and reassure his sons and followers that he knows what he is talking about. He had been to the seven heavens, had seen everything, and had talked with God Himself.

Good Christians take much comfort from Jesus' promise of the many mansions in his Father's house, where he would prepare a place for his disciples. They assume that Jesus meant not only those disciples he was speaking to at the Last Supper, but also all the saved and righteous Christians ever since. They do not expect unrighteous and unsaved sinners to have mansions or places in heaven: such people would have to go to hell.

So this verse in The Secrets of Enoch, which tells that in the Great Age to come there will be not only good mansions for the good people but bad ones without number for sinners, would not seem to agree with Jesus' belief, as expressed in John 14:2. In that verse, however, Jesus did not say that all the many mansions were for good folks only. He was going ahead of his disciples "to prepare a place" for them. What sort of "place" and why did he have to "prepare" it? This statement has usually been taken to mean that he would be preparing mansions for the righteous to live in, but in the light of the Enochan books and some Essenic scrolls, it may well be that he meant places at the Messianic Banquet, which the Last Supper apparently foreshadowed. There seems to be indicated here the idea of making reservations at an important feast where, in his Father's "house," he would act as host for his friends, his disciples.

Bible students will remember that the seating arrangements in the coming Messianic Age were much in the minds of the disciples, for James and John, the sons of Zebedee, bespoke for themselves the choicest seats: "Grant that we may sit, one on your right hand, the other on your left, in your glory" (Mark 10:37).

Jesus' answer was that to give special seats was not his privilege; such places were for those for whom they had already been prepared.

Here is a hint of predestination, with God assigning the seats at the Messianic Banquet—and doing it far in advance (before the foundation of the world, some said). This idea apparently assumes that God's powers are greater than those of Jesus. The same idea is found in Paul's First Letter to the Corinthians (15:28), which clearly states: ". . . then shall the Son also himself be subject unto him that put all things under him, that God may be all in all."

Scholars call this "an early type of Christology"— which, of course, it is. But in the light of the Scrolls, it is much more, for it reflects the thoughts and attitude of the man Jesus and of his early followers before the theologians made a god of him—a god who must have no other gods before him, and who certainly cannot be subject to any other god, not even to his own Heavenly Father. In other words, although both Jesus and Paul, in the latter's early epistles, conceived of Jesus' place as somewhat lower than that of God, later Christian theologians raised him to equality with God the Father, and eventually to the Second Person of the Trinity, making the Holy Ghost or Holy Spirit the Third Person.

But if it is God who assigns the seats at the Messianic Banquet, why did Jesus say he was going on ahead to prepare a place for his disciples?

Since most scholars have been accustomed to date John's Gospel as much later than Mark's, it could be argued that John 14:2,3, in which Jesus promises to prepare a place for his disciples, is an editorial correction of Mark 10:40, which speaks of such places as having already been prepared by God Himself. That is, the author of the Fourth Gospel (John's)—always keen to glorify Jesus—was already building him up in stature, even putting words in his mouth to counteract the statements quoted by Mark.

But now the Scrolls from the Essene caves (and, to a lesser extent and in a different way, the Chenoboskion Coptic codices) have led scholars to consider the Fourth Gospel (or its sources) of much earlier composition— perhaps as early as Mark. Thus there is apparently a flat contradiction in two reported sayings of Jesus. Such a contradiction between reporters is, of course, nothing unusual.

One could reconcile the contradictory assertions, however, by assuming that in John 14, Jesus meant by "a place for you" an abode, a dwelling, or, as the late and great Roman Catholic scholar, Father Knox, well put it, "a home." And when Jesus said to James and John (Mark 10:40), "but a place on my right hand or my left is not mine to give; it is for those for whom it has been destined," the "place" meant was a seat at the Messianic Banquet. Thus the first is a residence; the second, a reservation. Like the English word *place*, the Greek word *topos* used in John 14:2,3 can denote a place to live or a place to sit. And, at any rate, when we read in The Secrets of Enoch (61:2) that ". . . in the Great Age to come . . . many mansions are prepared for men . . . ," we immediately recognize the same thought that Jesus elaborated to comfort his disciples. And John (14:3) continues, "And if I go and prepare a place for you, I will come again, and receive you unto myself; that where I am, there ye may be also."

Jesus' admonition (according to Matthew 5:43-44), "Ye have heard that it hath been said, Thou shalt love thy neighbor, and hate thine enemy. But I say unto you, Love your enemies, bless them that curse you, do good to them that hate you . . . ," is reminiscent of The Secrets of Enoch (50:2-4): "Now then, my children, dwell in patience and peace . . . and every blow . . . and every

evil word . . . endure them; and although you may be
able to repay with interest, do not retaliate upon your
neighbor, since it is the Lord Who recompenses . . . ," or,
as another translation of the Slavonic Enoch puts it,
"When you might have vengeance, do not repay, either
your neighbor or your enemy."

The next verse in The Secrets of Enoch (50:5), "Lose
[spend] your gold and silver for your brother's sake,
and you will receive ample treasure [not of the carnal
kind] on the Day of Judgment," and the first verses of
the next chapter (51:1-2), "Extend your hands to the
orphan and the widow, and according to your ability help
the destitute, and they will prove to be like a shelter in
the time of storm," both remind the reader of the famous
saying of Jesus in Matthew 6:19-20: "Lay not up for
yourselves treasures upon earth, where moth and rust
doth corrupt. . . . But lay up for yourselves treasures in
heaven, where neither moth nor rust doth corrupt. . . ."

It may be, however, that both versions owe much to
the apocryphal book (written in Jerusalem about 180
B.C., by a teacher in a school there) variously called Ecclesiasticus, Sirach, or The Wisdom of Jesus, Son of
Sirach: "Lose thy money for thy brother and thy friend,
and let it not rust under a stone to be lost. Lay up thy
treasure according to the commandments of the most
High, and it shall bring thee more profit than gold"
(29:10-11).

One manuscript (called P by Bonwetsch and Vaillant, and A by R. H. Charles *) of the Enochan book has
an extra sentence in 51:2: "Save not (conceal not) your
silver in the earth." And, written above this section by
some unknown student is the sentence: "Enoch teaches
his sons that they should not hide treasure in the earth,
but bids them give alms to the poor." It is marked "Forty-
seventh Essay [or Discussion]." Evidently some Slavonic student or teacher had noted the similarity of this
section to another saying of Jesus, the parable of the

* See "Note" on first page of The Secrets of Enoch.

talents in Matthew 25:25, in which the unprofitable servant confesses: "I went and hid thy talent in the earth."

When Enoch was about to return to the heavens after
having told his sons of the glories he had seen on his
previous sojourn there, he said to them: "For lo! my
children, the appointed day approaches, and the set time
compels me. The angels who are going with me are here
waiting, and tomorrow I shall mount to the highest heaven
to my eternal inheritance. That is why, my children, I
am bidding you do before the face of the Lord all His
good pleasure" (55:1-3). Thereupon, he counseled them
at some length, blessed them, reminded them to clothe
the naked, to fill the hungry and to be kind to animals,
and (in chapter 61) mentioned the many mansions prepared for them in Paradise.

In strikingly similar fashion, the night before his crucifixion, "when Jesus knew that his hour was come that he
should depart out of this world unto the Father" (John
13:1), he gathered his disciples together in the upper
room for the Last Supper and said to them: "Little children, yet a little while I am with you. . . . Whither I go,
ye cannot come . . . but . . . follow me afterwards"
(John 13:33-36). He talked long with them, and it was
at this time that he told them of the many mansions he
was going to prepare for them (14:2).

There is still another noticeable—even conspicuous—
parallel in the two farewells. When Enoch told his sons
that he was obliged to leave them and go to the highest
heaven on the morrow, one of his sons, Mathusalem, suggested that a farewell banquet be given Enoch by all his
relatives, and that Enoch in turn bless them so that the
whole family might share in his fame and glory: "Would
it be pleasing to your eyes, father, if we made a meal
ready before you, that you might bless our houses and
your sons and all the folk of your household, and thereby
glorify your people [with you] before you depart?"
(56:1-2).

Possibly the author of The Secrets of Enoch was familiar with the Old Testament story of the aged Isaac's

request to his oldest son Esau: "Go out to the field and take me some venison; and make me some savory meat, such as I love, and bring it to me, that I may eat; that my soul may bless thee before I die" (Genesis 27:3-4). The blessing or utterance of a man at his last meal was presumed to be almost magically powerful, of the nature of a divine prophecy. The flesh of a freshly killed animal was apparently a necessary part of the meal, probably as a sacrifice to the deity. After Enoch had ascended with the angels to the highest heaven, Mathusalem and his brothers sacrificed sheep and cattle and had a three-day-long celebration with much merrymaking (68).

But when Mathusalem proposed the farewell meal, ". . . Enoch, answering his son, said, Listen, children, ever since the Lord had me anointed with the oil of His glory, there has been no food in me. In fact, food is not attractive to me, and I have no desire for earthly nourishment" (56:2).

Now, in the Gospel accounts of the Last Supper, Jesus, too, refused to eat or drink with his disciples. John's Gospel, for some reason, omits this point, but Matthew, Mark, and Luke all mention it, with slight variations. Luke records:

> "And when the hour had come, he sat down, and the apostles with him. And he said to them, I have greatly desired to eat this passover with you before I suffer; for, I say to you, I shall not eat it again until it is fulfilled in the kingdom of God. And he took a cup, and when he had given thanks, he said, 'Take this, and divide it among yourselves; for I say to you that henceforth I shall not drink of the fruit of the vine until the kingdom of God shall come' " (22:14-18).

Mark gives the last phrase as "until that day when I drink it new in the kingdom of God," but Matthew has it as "until that day when I drink it new with you in my Father's kingdom," which lends an intimate touch and a promise, like the personal warmth of the Last Supper discourse in John's Gospel.

A little later that night, Jesus was seized in the Garden of Gethsemane by "a great multitude with swords and clubs," and when Peter drew a sword to defend him, Jesus told him to put the sword back in its sheath and remarked, "Do you think I cannot now pray to my Father, and he will promptly send me more than twelve legions of angels?" (Matthew 26:53). Since the other Gospels do not mention Jesus' reference to the legions of angels, this verse has been assumed by some critics to have been interpolated later, or to have been added by the author to his sources. But elsewhere there are accounts of angels coming to help Jesus when he needed it. That very evening in Gethsemane, as Jesus prayed in agony of spirit, "there appeared an angel unto him from heaven, strengthening him" (Luke 22:43); and after Jesus' temptations in the wilderness, "angels came and ministered unto him" (Mark 1:13; Matthew 4:11).

And since no disciples were present at those three temptations in the wilderness, Jesus himself must have reported the presence of angels. So, whatever our own opinions about the existence of angels, we are led to suppose that Jesus believed in them.

Because there are so many parallels between the events and remarks during both Jesus' and Enoch's last evenings with their followers, there is probably additional correspondence in Enoch's remark, "the angels who are going with me are here waiting."

In the light of these various coincidences, is it too much to suppose that on his last night on earth Jesus had in mind at several times the story of the parting of Enoch from his children, and that—more or less consciously—he conformed his own conduct to that pattern?

CHAPTER 4
"But I Say Unto You"

There are in The Secrets of Enoch many little things —a concept, a word-image, a turn of phrase—which remind one of Jesus. They are elusive and sometimes hard to pin down. An inner conviction that one has come in contact with the mind of Jesus for a moment cannot always be reduced to a logical argument, but the feeling persists that whoever wrote the verse being read was someone whose thought and speech patterns were remarkably like his.

I have collected a number of these instances, and want to present a few of them—not because they are in themselves convincing evidence for our thesis, but because, in the light of the passages I have already given, they attain significance.

Take, for instance, the opening verse of chapter 42 of The Secrets of Enoch, where Enoch says, "I saw the keepers of the keys of hell, standing near the very high gates. . . ." Another manuscript has, "I saw the keyholders and guardians of the gates of hell standing. . . ."

Compare with that the well-known words of Jesus in

Matthew 16:18, 19 in the King James Version: "And I say also unto thee, That thou art Peter, and upon this rock I will build my church; and the gates of hell shall not prevail against it. And I will give unto thee the keys of the kingdom of heaven: and whatsoever thou shalt bind on earth shall be bound in heaven; and whatsoever thou shalt loose on earth shall be loosed in heaven." Several modern translations substitute "the powers" or "forces of death" for "the gates of hell," but the Latin Vulgate has "*portae inferi*" and the Greek says plainly "*pulai haidou*" (literally, "the gates of Hades"), and to change either to "the powers of death" is an unnecessary hermeneutic type of translation which destroys the accuracy and vigor of the original.

Of course, for those who do not believe in a literal hell, as Jesus apparently did, the gates of hell can be taken as a symbol of the powers of death, but the original imagery is better, and has persisted in literature and folklore ever since, so that even today people say, very expressively, "hot as the hinges of hell."

In comparing this passage in The Secrets of Enoch with the more famous one in Matthew, it should be noted that the Enochan verse refers to the keys of hell, but says nothing of the keys of heaven, whereas the reverse is true in the Matthean verse. Matthew does mention the gates of hell, but not the keys or the key-holders. Jesus did not promise to give Peter the keys to the gates of hell; those keys he apparently reserved for his own custody.

For in the Johannine Apocalypse, or Revelation, the author has a vision of the resurrected Jesus, who says, "I am he who died, but see, I am alive for evermore, and I have the keys of death and hell" (1:18). But, later on in the Apocalypse, the key-holder has changed: the King James Version reads, ". . . and I saw a star fall from heaven unto the earth; and to him was given the key of the bottomless pit" (Revelation 9:1). The American Standard Revised Version (1901) has it as "the key of the pit of the abyss," which makes little sense, and the recent Revised Standard Version (1946-52) isn't much better with "the key of the shaft of the bottomless pit."

Now this "star" of Revelation was, of course, an angel, as anyone familiar with the Enochan literature would know. This will be explained later, when the angelology of The Secrets of Enoch is compared with that of Jesus as given in the Gospels. It is sufficient here to point out that still further in the Apocalypse is found: "And I saw an angel come down from heaven having in his hand the key of the bottomless pit and a great chain" (20:1). This verse may be a repetition of 9:1, with the addition of the chain with which the angel proceeded to bind Satan, and then to "cast him into the bottomless pit, and shut him up, and set a seal upon him. . . ."

Since "the bottomless pit" was also called "the abyss" and had the same undesirable features, it is easily recognized as a surrogate for hell. And if the angel (Revelation 9, 20) had a key to unlock it, it must have had gates, so here again appear "the gates of hell," even if gates are not specifically mentioned. As a matter of fact, it looks as if a wrong word had crept into the text. The Greek word *phrear* usually means *well*, but it can also mean *pit* or *shaft*, and has been so interpreted by several translators. But it is hard to visualize the need of a key to a pit or abyss or hell without a lock and a door or gate. Certainly, the angel whose task it was to thrust Satan into the pit "and shut him up, and set a seal upon him" (Revelation 20:3), could hardly have done so unless there was a door or gate to shut and seal.

A passage in Matthew (16:18-19) quotes Jesus as saying that Peter was the "rock" upon which he would build his church, against which the gates of hell would not prevail, and that he would give Peter the keys of the kingdom of heaven, and that whatever Peter bound or loosed on earth would be bound or loosed in heaven. This is one of the most important passages in the New Testament and one of the best-known; its implications have been discussed by countless theologians, and their different interpretations still divide Christendom.

If Jesus said these words, it may well be that he took the Enochan conception of the key-holders and guardians of the gates of hell, and expanded and illuminated it into a picture so compelling that the Roman Catholic Church has chosen it as its symbol and guarantee of authority and power, claiming direct apostolic succession from Peter as the bishop of Rome and the first pope.

Protestants, however, take exception to that claim. They challenge the historicity of the alleged papal succession and even Peter's ever having been in Rome. They point out that Peter had no monopoly on the "binding and loosing," which is the basis of the Catholic claim to the sole right to forgive sins, for Jesus gave to all his disciples the same power of "binding and loosing" (Matthew 18:18), and made it even more definite, saying, "Whose soever sins ye forgive, they are forgiven . . ." (John 20:23).

Some scholars go much further. Dr. Henry B. Sharman of the University of Chicago, in his book, *The Teaching of Jesus About the Future*, gives twelve reasons for doubting that Jesus ever said to Peter the words in Matthew 16:17-19. It is certainly odd that both Mark 8:27-30 and Luke 9:18-21 have repeated Matthew 16:13-16 almost verbatim, and then Matthew 16:20, but give no parallel whatever for Matthew 16:17-19.

Furthermore, one saying of Jesus' has caused much perplexity among the believers in the Prince of Peace: "Think not that I am come to bring peace on earth: I have not come to bring peace, but a sword" (Matthew 10:34). In The Secrets of Enoch is written: "Woe to him who talks peace, but there is no peace in his heart" (52:14). And in one version of Enoch, the words "but a sword" appear. Prophetically, Jesus knew that his message was revolutionary and would cause divisions, even in united families, as the succeeding verses in Matthew admit. Jesus simply wanted it understood that he was no hypocrite, saying one thing and thinking another. He knew that his disciples would encounter conflict, and he was not deceiving them by promising them peace when he really knew in his heart that they were going to have a hard time. They would be hated by some when it was discovered that they were his followers. There is going to be real war between the Sons of Light and the Sons of Darkness, as Jesus may have learned at Qumran.

Yet Jesus counterbalanced this warning with another: "But I say unto you, That whosoever is angry with his brother without a cause shall be in danger of the judgment: and whosoever shall say to his brother, Raca, shall be in danger of the council, but whosoever shall say, Thou fool, shall be in danger of hell fire" (Matthew 5:22).

This pronouncement has puzzled earnest Bible students, Sunday School teachers, and great scholars for centuries, yet the key to the meaning of *Raca* is to be found in a parallel passage in The Secrets of Enoch.

In the King James Version, the meaning of *Raca* is given as *vain fellow*. The text of the Revised Standard Version (1959) has "whoever insults his brother," but admits in a footnote that the Greek has "says Raca to" (an obscure term of abuse). Other versions translate *Raca* as *pouring contempt, speaking contemptuously, saying, "You empty-headed fellow,"* or *calling someone a simpleton*. The last two interpretations—and several others, such as *vain fellow*—result from the attempt to derive *Raca* from the rabbinical Hebrew word *req*, meaning *empty*. That, however, is hard to justify, not only linguistically, but in the context, for *simpleton* or *vain fellow* is practically a synonym for *fool*, but in the next clause of the same verse the fool is mentioned and condemned to a much worse fate.

So *Raca* cannot mean simply *fool*. Nor can it have the other suggested meaning of mere contempt, for to be hailed before the High Council (Sanhedrin) simply for expressing scorn would have been ridiculous. Therefore, some worse offense is indicated.

Now chapter 44 of The Secrets of Enoch records a similar list of degrees of anger and insult with appropriate penalties. Unfortunately, the manuscripts of that chapter are full of variants, and it is difficult to know what the original really was. But there is fairly general agreement among the various translations of the manuscript group known as the Longer Redaction and among those of the Shorter Redaction; the translations of this passage really differ little in purport and general sense, and translators usually combine them.

For instance, W. R. Morfill was the first to translate into English the Slavonic manuscripts representing both redactions, and R. H. Charles edited and published Morfill's rather literal translation, which followed in the main the Longer Redaction (but not wholly), with the rather stilted result in the case of 44:1-3:

> "God made man with his own hands, in the likeness of His countenance, both small and great the Lord created him. He who reviles the countenance of man, reviles the countenance of the Lord. He who shows wrath against another without injury, the great wrath of the Lord shall consume him. If a man spits at the face of another insultingly, he shall be consumed in the great judgment of the Lord."

Professor Bonsirven's translation of *Hénoch II* (44:1-3), based principally on G. N. Bonwetsch's 1922 edition of *Die Bucher der Geheimnisse Henochs* (which contains carefully annotated texts of both redactions), is briefer and clearer than Morfill's. It is a little too free for accuracy, but carries the correct meaning. Here his French is translated into English:

> "Man was made in the image of God: to load with shame the face of man is to load with shame that of the Lord. He who gets angry with a man, without having been wronged, will reap the great anger of the Lord. He who spits in the face of a man will reap disgrace at the great judgment of the Lord."

The greatest punishment, then, is reserved for the man who spits in the face of his fellow man.

Now, in comparing any translation of The Secrets of Enoch 44:1-3 with Matthew 5:22, it is seen that the final insult, the calling a man a fool, for which the insulter is in danger of hell fire, is not found in The Secrets of Enoch, nor is hell fire mentioned. But when the final insult is dropped from the Matthean verse, the climactic word *Raca* parallels the Enochan spitting insult.

So it is obvious that *Raca* has something to do with spitting. What is the Hebrew (or Aramaic) word for *spitting?* The act is mentioned in several places in the Old Testament—in Numbers (12:14) and Deuteronomy (25:9) the Hebrew word is *yaraq;* in Leviticus (15:8) it is *raqaq.* The noun *spittle* in Job (7:19) is *roq.* All these are close enough to *Raca* (which is spelled in various translations as *Racha, raka, rakka, raccha*) to warrant the inference that to say *Raca* meant to say *I spit on you,* if not actually to spit.

Moreover, Jesus was speaking in Aramaic, a sort of early Hebrew dialect, and *raka* was probably the nearest Greek spelling of the original Aramaic; when the Greek was translated into English, the word became *Raca.*

This conjecture finds further support in George M. Lamsa's introduction to *The Gospels from Aramaic,* in which he emphasizes the difficulties of translating certain Aramaic words into Greek, for in Aramaic a single word may have many meanings and the misplacing of a dot may change the meaning altogether. "Furthermore," he says, "some Aramaic words were not translated into Greek because they were not clearly understood. Such words are *rakah, to spit. . . .*"

But why does spitting merit so severe a punishment both in Matthew's Gospel and in The Secrets of Enoch? In the Manual of Discipline, the rules of the Qumran community, anyone "spitting in the midst of the session of the Many" was only fined (i.e., deprived of one fourth of his food allowance for thirty days).

The answer lies in the difference in degree of offense.

Spitting in the meeting of the Assembly was a misdemeanor, an unsanitary act; spitting, or threatening to spit, in the face of a fellow man, was an insult both to man and to God, in whose image man is made. Moreover, it was a sin of anger, and even an evidence of hatred.

Recently, an American ballplayer was heavily fined for spitting toward some heckling fans in the bleachers. And when *Life* interviewed some refugees who had suffered at the hands of Adolf Eichmann and asked them what should be done to him, one Roumanian refugee was quoted as saying, "They should not execute Eichmann. He should walk the streets so people could spit on him."

In other words, in this man's opinion it would be worse than death for the criminal to be forced to run the gantlet of outraged people spitting their contempt and hatred on him.

More poignantly we can realize now how much Jesus loathed to see (as he must have frequently seen) an angry man spitting vindictively in another's face, and how he ranked it as one of the worst of insults. How keenly he must have suffered in spirit at the last when "they did spit in his face, and buffeted him and slapped him." Four places in the canonical Gospels (Matthew 26:67 and 27:30; Mark 14:65 and 15:19) tell of the horrible spitting upon Jesus.

Yet, we can well imagine him recalling through all the tortured hours of his trial—perhaps repeating softly to himself for solace and strength—the words of the Suffering Servant described in Isaiah, admired so much at Qumran, and whom Jesus himself apparently took as one of his models:

> "I have set my face as a flint, and I know that I shall not be ashamed. . . . I have not turned away. . . . I gave my back to those who smote me, and turned my cheeks to those who pulled out the hairs: nor did I hide my face from shame and spitting" (Isaiah 50:5-7).

It may be significant that in both Enoch and Matthew the verses about the sin of anger are followed by a short section about sacrifices and the proper attitude of the worshiper before the altar. The author of The Secrets of Enoch goes on to say, "Is it that the Lord has need of offerings of bread, or candles, or sheep, or cattle? (These are nothing: He desires a pure heart.) But with these He tests the heart of man" (45:3). Similarly, in Matthew, Jesus follows his warnings about anger with: "Therefore if thou bring thy gift to the altar, and there rememberest that thy brother hath aught against thee [for having said *Raca* to him, for instance]; Leave there thy gift before the altar, and go thy way; first be reconciled to thy brother, and then come and offer thy gift" (5:23,24).

The Matthean version is clearer and more cogent, but the Enochan passage certainly contains the same message and breathes the same spirit. The sequence of the anger-sacrifice sections, with the Lord's Great Judgment Day always in the background, might well be one indication that the same mind, with its characteristic thought-patterns, created both passages.

In the Sermon on the Mount, as recorded by Matthew, Jesus says, "Swear not at all; neither by heaven; . . . nor by the earth; . . . neither by Jerusalem; . . . neither . . . by thy head; . . . but let thy communication be Yea, yea; Nay, nay; for whatsoever is more than these cometh of evil" (5:34-37). Many good Christians have refused to take an oath in a law court because of this command.

In The Secrets of Enoch we read: ". . . I will not swear by any oath, neither by the heaven nor by the earth, nor by any other creation of the Lord . . . and if among men there is no truth, let them swear with a single word: yea, yes, or else, no, no" (49:1).

Certainly this verse in the Enochan book bears a striking similarity to the passage in Matthew. The reader is almost forced to conclude either that Jesus was quoting the words of someone else in his Sermon on the Mount or that he was repeating in slightly better form his own previously written words. If they were his own words, there was no need for him to acknowledge their source. But if he was quoting from some other author, it would have been natural for him to preface the words with an acknowledgment, such as "As Enoch saith . . ." or "as it hath been said . . ."—particularly since in the preceding sentence he had made just such an acknowledgment of another quotation: "Again, ye have heard that it hath been said to them of old time, Thou shalt not forswear [perjure] thyself, but shalt fulfill thine oaths unto the Lord . . ." (Matthew 5:33). Then comes "But I say unto you, Swear not at all . . ." (Matthew 5:34).

If verse 33 is supposed to be an exact quotation from the Old Testament, it cannot be identified in modern Bibles. It seems, rather, to be a rather clever summary of several verses in the Law of Moses (the Torah) which have a similar meaning (Exodus 20:7, Leviticus 19:12, Deuteronomy 5:11, 23:21-23, and Numbers 30:2).

Here is another little link between Jesus and the Qumran community, for this summary and blending of several passages from the Torah into one statement is characteristic of the Dead Sea communitarians. Such a combination of quotations, cleverly integrated and focused, was a literary device popular at Qumran, and, if not invented there, was developed and perfected in the writings, as certain discovered manuscripts show. It has been dubbed by scholars a *florilegium* (roughly translatable as *a bouquet of sayings*).

Florilegium or not, and no matter who commanded the ancients not to *break* oaths, there can be no doubt that Jesus improved the ethics by telling his disciples not to *make* oaths, and claimed to be the first to do so. He distinctly states he is the original author of the words in Matthew (5:34-37), for he begins the passage by saying, "But I say unto you . . ." Yet these words are also found, as we have seen, in The Secrets of Enoch.

Now this book was written between A.D. 1 and 50, as scholars have maintained. That was before any of the Gospels was written, and even before Jesus began his public ministry. So, the author of this passage could not have been quoting from Matthew's Gospel.

We seem then to be driven to the conclusion that Jesus was repeating and emphasizing as his own original thought this pronouncement on oaths which he had previously written in the Enochan book. This single passage is sufficient to suggest the possibility, even the probability, of Jesus' authorship of The Secrets of Enoch, but the theory is strengthened by still other interesting parallels between that book and the Gospels. Indeed, one who knows and loves the words of Jesus cannot read the Enochan book without noting that many of the words and phrases are peculiar to the Nazarene.

Bible students who have read these few pages on oaths may say, "But what about the Epistle of James?" It is true that James, who was the brother of Jesus, writes: "But above all things, my brethren, swear not, neither by heaven, neither by the earth, neither by any other oath: but let your yea be yea, and your nay, nay; lest ye come under condemnation" (James 5:12). Whether this passage was gleaned from Matthew, Enoch, the Agrapha or the oral tradition is not known. It seems to resemble the Enochan version most closely, and since the discovery of the Qumran literature, the whole Epistle of James is now seen to be more Essene than Christian, for most scholars now admit that the Enochan books had their provenance among the Essenes.

CHAPTER 5

From the Highest Heaven

For the Jews in the days of Jesus, the world was one of unrelieved evil, visible and invisible. They had been subjected and ruled by the cruel tyrants of Assyria, Egypt, Babylon, Greece and Rome, and the bloodthirsty reign of Herod the Great was horrifyingly fresh in their minds. There seemed to be no end to their suffering, and the very air was full of malicious, hostile spirits. But good angels had once visited and guided their forefathers, and their belief and reliance in Yahweh was unshakable. He was just and merciful, and His chosen people longed and prayed for the promised advent of the Messiah, when righteousness would triumph in the dawn of the millennium (as described by The Secrets of Enoch), or in the glory of eternal life in the City of God.

It was this undying hope of ultimate justice and equity that underlay the popularity of the apocalyptic literature, which was concerned with the phenomena of "last things" on earth. This inspiring outlook produced a great wealth and variety of writings during the several hundred years between Malachi and Matthew. Its origin may be traced to Isaiah (24-27) and Ezekiel (27). Later, Zechariah and Joel took up the eschatological theme, and Daniel (7) brought it to a climax in his depiction of the Last Judgment. (It is a wonder that Daniel was ever admitted into the canon of the Old Testament, for the orthodox Jewish hierarchy frowned on and discouraged the reading of apocalyptic literature. However, the people loved its message of comfort and courage, and "bootlegged" the manuscripts.)

It is clear that Jesus shared with his compatriots the belief that the wicked world was due for imminent destruction. After his baptism in the River Jordan by John the Baptist, he began his ministry in Galilee with John's urgent call: "Repent, for the Kingdom of Heaven is at hand." (It is important to note that this decisive event in the life of Jesus took place not many miles away from Qumran monastery.) Were these two young men influenced by the Essenes? Since the discovery of the Dead Sea Scrolls, many scholars have detected indications of such an influence. One indication may be this peculiar immersion of the body, in such ceremony by the Essene sect.

Also, the Essene doctrine contained its own selected hosts of angels and demons, as witnessed in the official documents preserved in the unearthed scrolls. Could it be significant that after his baptism Jesus retired into the Judean Desert for forty days, was tempted by Satan, defeated him, and was administered to by celestial angels? (Mark 1:13).

But, indeed, devils and angels were destined to play critical roles in his mortal existence, from birth to death, as well as in his immortal life, from the resurrection to ascension. He cast out devils from the sick, the evil ones sometimes recognizing him in hatred. Shining angels hovered over the Bethlehem stable and appeared in his tomb.

Countless such spirits of good and evil are described and classified by the author of The Secrets of Enoch;

they are eternally busy in the seven heavens he is taken to, and out of which Satan (an archangel whose name there was Satanail) had been "hurled" by God for conspiring to equal Him. Thus loosed in the universe, Satan takes his revenge for his downfall on man. God tells Enoch that this rebel archangel and his banned legions fly ceaselessly over an unfathomable abyss of space.

The Almighty not only commands that His summoned guest be clad in glorious raiment and shown His seven heavens, but takes him into His confidence and tells him why and how He is going to destroy (by means of the Flood) the world He created, as Divine retribution for its sinfulness (Second Enoch, 65:1-10; 70:3,6,9,23). The Lord also speaks of His Second Coming (the first being at the time of Creation), and warns that humans will always be wicked, and will spring from the progeny of the few He has planned to save from the Deluge.

The Almighty also goes on to tell Enoch all about how He created the world and man. In this recital of the events of the week of Creation, God relates how he discovered Adam's sin and therefore banished him from Paradise: "I said: You are earth, and you will go into that same earth from which I took you. I shall not annihilate you, but I shall send you to the place whence I took you: then I shall be able to take you again at the time of My second coming" (Second Enoch 32:1).

Some scholars have taken this reference to a Second Coming as an indication of Christian tampering with the text, either by editing or interpolating, to make a Jewish book prophesy the Christian doctrine of the Second Advent of Christ, just as Matthew quotes various relevant or adaptable Old Testament passages as prophecies of the acts and words of Jesus.

But whatever connection there may have been between the parousias (appearances), first or second, of God and Jesus, it is perfectly apparent that this verse in The Secrets of Enoch has reference to the Second Coming of God Himself, a belief current among the Jews before and during the lifetime of Jesus.

To the Jews the First Coming occurred at the time of the Creation and, as Dr. James Moffatt shows in the *Encyclopedia of Religion and Ethics,* the Second Coming would occur on the Day of Judgment (referred to many times in the Old Testament as the Day of the Lord, when God would appear and judge all men).

A belief of postexilic Judaism was that God would send ahead or bring with Him a Messiah or a Son of Man to help with the judging or even to take over the whole task. But the relatively late pseudepigraphical book, the Assumption of Moses (written between A.D. 7 and 30), contains the following passage: "For the Most High will arise, the Eternal God alone, and He will make His appearance to punish the Gentiles . . ." (10:7).

By the end of the first century A.D., the Jewish Ezra Apocalypse (Fourth Ezra) attempted to prove (chapter 6) that "The End of the Age [the Last Judgment] Shall Come by the Agency of God Alone." The author explains and connects the First and Second Comings. When Ezra asks God through whom or by whom He would again visit His creation, He replies:

"Before even the heavenward portals were standing, or even the wind blasts blew, when the foundations of paradise were not yet laid, nor the beauty of its flowers [the stars] yet seen, . . . even then I had all these things planned in My mind; through Me alone and no other were they created; and also the End [shall come] through Me alone and none other."

The emphasis is clearly on the fact that the God who alone was responsible for the Creation would bring about the end of Creation without any assistant or intermediary, whether Messiah, Son of Man, Logos, or Christian Christ. This beautiful passage in the Ezra Apocalypse was obviously composed by an orthodox rabbinic Jewish writer to confute and counteract both the sectarian Essene teaching of the coming of the Son of Man to judge the world, and the related and perhaps derived Christian teaching then being proclaimed: that the risen Jesus was the Christ or Messiah, the Son of Man, and that his Second Coming to judge the world was soon to take place. The Christians held that the First Coming was the Incarnation, when God became man in Jesus, an event which was variously placed at the time of his conception by Mary, at the time of his birth, or at the time of his baptism by John in Jordan.

The transformation of the Jewish conception of the Second Coming of God into the Christian conception of the Second Coming of Jesus Christ took place among Judeo-Christians during the first century A.D.—perhaps during the lifetime of Jesus, and quite possibly in his own thinking.

Any Christian who knows how important the idea of this Second Coming became to Jesus toward the end of his life will immediately recognize the significance of the first verse of chapter 32 of The Secrets of Enoch, in which God tells Adam how He is going to come and take him again at His Second Coming. Also clear is the relation of that Enochan verse to John 14:3, in which Jesus tells his disciples how he is going to receive them unto himself at his Second Coming.

Students of the inner mind of Jesus have long wondered how he first got the idea that he was to return to earth. There have been several theories, all related to what is usually referred to as his Messianic consciousness, but it may well be that there lies here a clue to a deeper motivation.

As Jesus approached the climax of his life, he became aware of his inevitably approaching death and grew more conscious of his close relationship to his Heavenly Father. In chapter 10 of the Gospel of John, Jesus is quoted as saying, "I and the Father are one," and in chapter 14, "he that hath seen me hath seen the Father." These statements have been much discussed by theologians. They may be interpreted as the fruits of oriental exaggeration whether they are verbatim quotations or colored by the Evangelist's memory and vocabulary.

Furthermore, since both statements were apparently made under considerable emotional tension, they are probably more important psychologically than theologically. But, whatever the exegesis, exposition or explanation, it can be assumed that as Jesus saw his end was near, he had a growing feeling of closeness to God, his Heavenly Father. And even if he knew that his Heavenly Father was his own projected ideal self (which may have been what he was trying to tell his disciples), it is still a natural inference that his feeling of a "closer walk with God"—of rapprochement or harmonious intimacy with his Divine Maker—would naturally lead him to act as he presumed his God would act. He would assume the characteristic attitude he supposed his Eternal Father would take toward men.

God expected to come again and take Adam, the typical totemic man, back to the heavens with Him at His Second Coming. What, then, was more natural than that Jesus, strongly conscious of his closeness to God, should appropriate for himself that role and assure his disciples that he would come back to earth and take them back to the heavens with him to the mansions that he would have prepared for them?

So much in Enoch's book illuminates the inner life of the Nazarene, that it sometimes seems as though it might well be named the Book of the Secrets of Jesus.

If, as I am inclined to suspect, Jesus wrote The Secrets of Enoch—or part of it—some time during those eighteen silent years before he began his public ministry, and before the message he was to bring to the world had become clear to him, the coincidence between many passages in the book and the later teachings of his maturity would be explainable. The Gospel quotations are usually more rounded and polished, but the Enochan passages provide a glimpse into Jesus' mind in the making, a sort of insight into the earlier stages of his philosophy of life. And this preview, as it were, of the processes of thought which were to result in his moral, ethical, social and religious pronouncements, allows us to fill in certain gaps and to clarify obscure places in the incomplete and sometimes vague accounts of that teaching as recorded by the Gospel writers. As passages in this hitherto neglected work are compared with the familiar New Testament records, it becomes more and more apparent that The Secrets of Enoch has in it much of what we should expect to find if Jesus had written it, say, in his early twenties at Qumran.

The writing of such a book might have been a prescribed literary exercise for the students at the Essene community of Qumran. The more the remains of that settlement are studied, the more it is seen to have resembled a college rather than the monastery or monkish retreat that scholars first took it to be. In Cave 4 alone, portions of ten different manuscripts of Enoch were found, each differing in some respects from the others, and from the Ethiopic and Slavonic Enochs. In several of the many caves, other fragments were found, to say nothing of the many apocryphal booklets evidently based on and elaborating the older Enochan books.

This body of Enochan and semi-Enochan literature corroborates what was hitherto suspected by a few scholars working in the field of the pseudepigrapha: that there were numerous books of Enoch. The Qumran discoveries point to the fact that the so-called Ethiopic Enoch, containing at least five Enochan books written by several men at different times, and the Slavonic Enoch are only evidence of a once vast Enochan literature. Much of this literature has been destroyed by time; but more has been destroyed by fanatical orthodox defenders of the faith, who decided to eliminate these dangerous apocalyptic writings, so disturbingly similar to the teachings of Jesus.

If, then, the cave discoveries have revealed (and keep on revealing) new variants of Enoch and of Enochan ideas and teachings, what more natural than to suspect that at the Qumran college the students were expected, as part of their training, to compose literary religious essays and theses telling of Enoch's visit to the seven heavens and the secrets he learned there from God and the angels? So, if The Secrets of Enoch closely resembles, in language and thought patterns, the teachings and doctrines of Jesus as these are recorded in the Gospels, we are certainly dutybound to explore further the probability that Jesus tried his hand at composing a Book of Enoch, as a pedagogical duty or as a self-imposed task.

Jesus described to his disciples rather graphically, even dramatically, what would happen at his Second Coming. When the Son of Man came in his glory, he would sit on his throne, and separate the evil people from the good, placing the good ones on his right hand:

> "Then shall the King say unto them on his right hand, Come, ye blessed of my Father, inherit the kingdom prepared for you from the foundation of the world: For I was an hungered, and ye gave me meat: I was thirsty, and ye gave me drink: I was a stranger, and ye took me in: Naked, and ye clothed me: I was sick, and ye visited me: I was in prison, and ye came unto me" (Matthew 25:31-36).

The righteous, in some surprise, would then ask the King when all this had happened, and he would reply that when they had done one of these kind deeds "unto the least of these my brethren" they had done it unto him. The same procedure would be followed with the evil persons who failed to minister to the King because they had not been kind to "the least of these." To these he would say: "Depart from me, ye cursed, into everlasting fire, prepared for the devil and his angels" (Matthew 25:41). "And these shall go away into everlasting punishment: but the righteous into life eternal" (Matthew 25:46).

These last sixteen verses of Matthew 25 are simply the expansion and elaboration of a single long verse in chapter 9 of The Secrets of Enoch. In chapter 8, Enoch reaches the third heaven, in which are sweet-flowering trees and springs of honey and milk, oil and wine, in a garden kept by three hundred sweetly singing angels. This is Paradise, and Enoch says, "What a very splendid place this is!" His angel guides then say to him,

> "This place, O Enoch, is prepared for the righteous, who, in their lifetime, endure troubles which distress their souls; yet they avoid iniquity, judge others fairly, give bread to the hungry, cover with their own robe the naked, lift up the fallen, help the wronged, and walk blameless in the sight of the Lord. It is for these that this place is prepared for an eternal inheritance" (9:1).

Note that the striking similarities of these two passages are not confined to the feeding of the hungry and the clothing of the naked; both the Matthean and the Enochan accounts contain the words *prepared, righteous, inherit* and *eternal.*

It might be thought that the Enochan passage contains one phrase indicating a slightly higher ethic than its Matthean counterpart, for those who "cover with their *own* robe the naked" show more personal consideration than those referred to in "naked, and ye clothed me." But perhaps the Matthean passage which quotes Jesus as saying, "And if any man will sue thee at the law and take away thy coat, let him have thy cloak also" (5:40), exhibits even greater unselfishness.

Although Enoch 9:1 says nothing about the wicked being sent to hell for failing to feed the hungry and clothe the naked as does Matthew 25:41, he gives that side of the picture even more vividly later.

The angel guides lead Enoch to the "northern side" of the same third heaven in which Paradise is located, and there show him a "very terrible place" where "all is agony and torment, darkness and mist," where "there is no light save a dim fire which keeps flaring up. A fiery stream moves close by . . . yet cold and ice are there;

and in the dungeons angels bearing rude and sharp instruments torture without mercy" (10:1-3). The guides explain to Enoch that the persons thus suffering are there because of various sins. Among the listed crimes are "letting the starving die although able to feed them well, and stripping the needy naked when they could clothe them. . . ."

No one who reads Enoch 9 and 10 and then reads Matthew 25:31-46 can fail to be impressed with the similarity of thought and expression in the two.

If we admit the striking similarity between the Matthean and Enochan accounts of the Last Judgment, one of three conclusions is possible: (1) Jesus did not say what Matthew says he did—and, indeed, Matthew is suspected of adding a bit to his sources here and there; (2) Jesus was quoting from the earlier source without credit, probably knowing that his hearers were familiar with the Enochan book; or (3) Jesus was introducing into his dramatic account of the coming Day of Judgment, a part of the vivid description of Paradise and hell which he himself had previously written in The Secrets of Enoch. What other conclusion is possible?

In Enoch 8, 9 and 10 is the solution to a problem which has long puzzled Bible students. Jesus, in a story attributed to him in Luke 16, tells of a righteous beggar who died and "was carried by the angels into Abraham's bosom"—that is, he was given the place of honor next to Abraham at the heavenly feast of the righteous. According to the parable, there also died a rich man who had "fared sumptuously every day" and the crumbs from whose table the poor starving Lazarus had often begged. The rich man went to hell, evidently because he had failed to feed the hungry. This parable, like so many of Jesus' teachings, fits right in the Enochan frame of reference.

Now the puzzling thing for a modern reader of the story is the fact that the rich man, while he was tormented by thirst in hell, was nevertheless able to see and to converse with Abraham in heaven and to beg him to send Lazarus with a drop of water to cool his hot tongue. The conversation went on for some time (Luke 16:19-31), and Christians have wondered how hell could be so close to the heavenly feast. Apparently, although Abraham was "afar off" and between him and the rich man there was "a great gulf fixed," there could not have been too great a distance between heaven and hell, or the long dialogue could not have occurred. (It looks as if the phrases "afar off" and "great gulf" may have been inserted in the story by a later editor who didn't approve of such proximity as Jesus and the Enochan writer indicated.)

This was a communication problem which never occurred to Jesus, for his conception of the heavens was exactly that of the author of The Secrets of Enoch, whose Paradise and hell, as we have seen, are both in the third heaven, with hell simply on the "northern side."

Nor would the Apostle Paul have been concerned overmuch with this point, for he was very familiar with the Enochan literature and the Essene conception of the seven heavens; he even claimed (Second Corinthians 12:1-12) to have been translated, like Enoch, and taken "as far as the third heaven" and then into its Paradise. In this dream vision Paul, like Enoch, heard sacred secrets, not to be revealed to mortals. Whether these "unspeakable" revelations were all given to him in the Paradise part of the third heaven, or whether he was taken into the northern side or hell, he does not say. However, he does tell us (Second Corinthians 12:2-3) that "I knew a man in Christ above fourteen years ago" who was "caught up into Paradise and heard unspeakable words, which is not lawful for a man to utter." And he goes on to say that he was given "a thorn in the flesh, a Satanic messenger to torment me continually" (12:7). Was this the "thorn" about which theologians have conjectured and debated for centuries?

Both Jesus and Paul, then, were well acquainted with the experience of Enoch in the seven heavens, as these were related in The Secrets of Enoch. If modern Bible students knew more of these "secrets," they would more fully understand the teachings of Jesus and the Epistles of Paul. It cannot be too often stressed that the thought-world of Jesus and Paul was the same as that of the author of The Secrets of Enoch.

In the much debated Epistle to the Hebrews (its authorship has been variously credited to Paul, an Alexandrian Jew, Apollos, and an unknown woman), Jesus is presented as a great high priest exalted above all the *heavens* (4:14). The concept of the plurality of the next world goes back to immemorial times, and the ancient peoples had a deep, mystical feeling about the indivisible number seven.

For the Jews, the number seven takes its religious significance from Genesis, in which God declared the seventh day of His Creation labors to be the holy Sabbath, a day of rest. Moderns have scoffed at this time limit, but those "days" were then reckoned at one thousand years each, and the one of "rest" prefigured a future millennium of workless bliss, according to the divinely informed Enoch.

Babylonians and Persians also had their doctrines of the seven heavens. The Babylonians even divided hell into seven parts. Again, Zoroastrianism postulated seven heavens, in the highest of which sat Zarathustra on a golden throne. The Koran adopted the same concept (probably borrowed from The Secrets of Enoch in its wanderings): "And we have created over you seven heavens" (Sura 23); "And we formed them into seven heavens in two days, and revealed unto every heaven its office" (Sura 41). The Koran also borrows Enoch's four streams of Paradise flowing with honey, milk, oil and wine (Sura 47).

Finally, Canon Charles said, "In the Slavonic Enoch, so far as I am aware, the most elaborate account of the seven heavens in any language is found."

CHAPTER 6

Multiplied Beatitudes and "Woes"

One of the most arresting parallels between The Secrets of Enoch and the Gospel record of the sayings of Jesus is found in the beatitudes.

Strangely, the word *beatitude* never occurs in the English Bible, but the Latin *beatitudo* of Jerome's Vulgate version, used in churches for many centuries, was adopted and adapted as *beatitudes* to serve as the noun in place of the awkward *blessèds*. But *beatitude* is not exact enough for scholars (it has other meanings, such as *a state of felicity*), so they have chosen to use *macarism*, from the Greek *makarismos* (a noun derived from the adjective *makario*s, the very word used in the Greek New Testament for *beatitudes*).

Every Christian is supposed to be familiar with the Nine Beatitudes of Jesus which begin chapter 5 of Matthew's Gospel. Sunday School children are (or were) required to memorize them, along with the Ten Commandments, the Lord's Prayer, and several favorite psalms. The position of the beatitudes, at the beginning of Jesus'

Sermon on the Mount, indicates the importance they held in the mind of the compiler of Matthew's Gospel—and all Christendom has agreed with him.

The beatitudes, as given in the King James Version (Matthew 5:1-12) are as follows:

> "And seeing the multitudes, he went up into a mountain: and when he was set, his disciples came unto him: and he opened his mouth and taught them, saying,
>
> "Blessed are the poor in spirit: for theirs is the kingdom of heaven.
>
> "Blessed are they that mourn: for they shall be comforted.
>
> "Blessed are the meek: for they shall inherit the earth.
>
> "Blessed are they which do hunger and thirst after righteousness: for they shall be filled.
>
> "Blessed are the merciful: for they shall obtain mercy.
>
> "Blessed are the pure in heart: for they shall see God.
>
> "Blessed are the peacemakers: for they shall be called the children of God.
>
> "Blessed are they which are persecuted for righteousness' sake: for theirs is the kingdom of heaven.
>
> "Blessed are ye, when men shall revile you, and persecute you, and shall say all manner of evil against you falsely, for my sake. Rejoice, and be exceeding glad: for great is your reward in heaven: for so persecuted they the prophets which were before you."

When, as a child, I had memorized the beatitudes, I was much surprised and a little disturbed to discover another, quite different version of them in Luke:

> "[Jesus] went out into a mountain to pray, and continued all night in prayer to God. And when it

was day, he called unto him his disciples, and of them he chose twelve, whom also he named apostles. . . . And he came down with them, and stood in the plain. . . . And a great multitude of people . . . came to hear him, and to be healed of their diseases; . . . and they were healed. . . .

"And he lifted up his eyes on his disciples, and said,

"Blessed be ye poor; for yours is the kingdom of God.

"Blessed are ye that hunger now: for ye shall be filled.

"Blessed are ye that weep now: for ye shall laugh.

"Blessed are ye, when men shall hate you, and when they shall separate you from their company, and shall reproach you, and cast out your name as evil, for the Son of man's sake. Rejoice ye in that day, and leap for joy: for, behold, your reward is great in heaven: for in the like manner did their fathers unto the prophets.

"But woe unto you that are rich! for ye have received your consolation.

"Woe unto you that are full! for ye shall hunger.

"Woe unto you that laugh now! for ye shall mourn and weep.

"Woe unto you, when all men shall speak well of you! for so did their fathers to the false prophets" (Luke 6:12-13, 17-18, 20-26).

So, instead of nine beatitudes, Luke had only four, and, along with the "blessèds" there were these four strange woes or "cursèds." Moreover, the Lukan beatitudes were much blunter and more materialistic in their content. One of my college professors termed them socialistic, noting that instead of "Blessed are the poor in spirit," Luke had "Blessed be ye poor," and in place of "Blessed are they which do hunger and thirst after righteousness," he had "Blessed are ye that hunger now."

Nowadays the professors who have studied the Qumran Scrolls are apt to implement the "socialistic" idea by saying that the Lukan beatitudes and woes are colored, more obviously than Matthew's, by anticipation of the expected imminent coming of the Messianic Kingdom.

When I first read The Secrets of Enoch, I found, in chapter 42, a set of nine beatitudes. I noted that they somewhat represented the beatitudes of Jesus, but dismissed the fact as an interesting coincidence. As I read on, I found in chapter 52 seven more "blesseds" alternating with seven associated "curseds." Even this seemed no more than another coincidence, but later, in the light of the many other parallels I discovered, these "coincidences" became significant.

Now, beatitudes are not a very common literary form; they are definitely and especially associated with Jesus. Although he did not originate that method of conveying moral and spiritual precepts, he certainly improved and popularized it. When the beatitudes of Jesus are mentioned, most people think merely of the most familiar ones: those in Matthew 5 and Luke 6.

But many more of Jesus' beatitudes have been preserved in other parts of the New Testament and in the non-biblical scriptures—and some of them, at least, are as high in quality as any of those in Matthew and Luke. Take the Isolated Beatitudes, the single sayings found in Matthew, Luke and John:

"Blessed is he, whosoever shall not be offended in me" (Matthew 11:6). (Luke 7:23 has the same.)

"Blessed are your eyes, for they see: and your ears, for they hear" (Matthew 13:16). (Luke 10:23 has "Blessed are the eyes which see the things that ye see.")

"Blessed art thou, Simon Bar-Jona: for flesh and blood hath not revealed it unto thee, but my Father which is in heaven" (Matthew 16:17).

"Blessed are they that hear the word of God, and keep it" (Luke 11:28).

"Blessed are those servants whom the Lord when

he cometh shall find watching" (Luke 12:37; see also Luke 12:43 and Matthew 24:46).

"But when thou makest a feast, call the poor, the maimed, the lame, the blind: And thou shalt be blessed; for they cannot recompense thee: for thou shalt be recompensed at the resurrection of the just" (Luke 14:13-14).

"If ye know these things, happy are ye if ye do them" (John 13:17).

"Blessed are they that have not seen, and yet have believed" (John 20:29).

We are indebted to Paul for an otherwise unknown beatitude of Jesus', for in Acts 20:35 he says, "I have showed you how in all things you should labor to support the weak, remembering the words of the Lord Jesus, how he said, "It is more blessed to give than to receive."

Again, one fifth-century manuscript of the Gospels, Codex Bezae, is unique in preserving another of Jesus' beatitudes. In Codex Bezae, Luke 6:5, in which Jesus said, "The Son of Man is Lord also of the Sabbath," is followed by:

> "On the same day, seeing one working on the Sabbath, He said unto him, O man, if indeed thou knowest what thou doest, thou art blessed; but if thou knowest not, thou art accursed and a transgressor of the law."

Note that this quotation presents again the Luke 6 alternation of blessing and cursing, which seems to be rather characteristic of Jesus' teaching. It is best shown, perhaps, in Matthew 25:31-46, where in a very apocalyptical passage, Jesus tells the coming fate of the "sheep" and the "goats," the sheep being those good people who fed the hungry, clothed the naked, and visited the sick and the imprisoned; the goats, those who did not. When the Son of Man comes in his glory and the angels with him, he will say to the sheep: "Come, ye blessed of my

Father, inherit the kingdom prepared for you from the foundation of the world," but to the goats he would say: "Depart from me, ye cursed, into everlasting fire, prepared for the devil and his angels."

Some Bible students have wondered why Matthew did not include the woes which Luke lists. But Matthew records elsewhere fourteen woes pronounced by Jesus; seven of these are scattered through chapters 11, 18, 24 and 26, and seven are included in chapter 23, in which he excoriates the lawyers and Pharisees. Mark has only two woes, but Luke repeats them, together with the Matthean diatribes against the lawyers and Pharisees. These, with the four woes which follow the four beatitudes in chapter 6, are the sixteen woes or "cursèds" Luke records as having been pronounced by Jesus.

Jesus' own words, as recorded in the Gospels, and its popularity among the Essenes of Qumran indicate that one of Jesus' favorite Old Testament books was Deuteronomy. It may be from Deuteronomy 28, in which six beatitudes and six "cursèds" appear, that he originally got the idea of balancing the two.

But the Deuteronomic blessings and curses are different—more in the nature of primitive magic spells cast by holy men and priests to bring good or bad luck. As in so many of his teachings, Jesus improved upon what was said "by them of old." The whole Sermon on the Mount (Matthew 5-7), including the beatitudes, is a collection of the many improvements in morals and customs, Jewish and Essenic, taught by Jesus—not to destroy the Law and the Prophets, but to extend, improve and complete the code of ethics.

The number of beatitudes created by Jesus has been greatly underestimated, because many of them have been attributed to other men. Of course, in some cases it is hard to tell whether the author is quoting from the sayings of Jesus in written or oral sources, or whether he has composed (or altered) the beatitude himself.

Again, there have been many translation slips between the cup of the Greek language and the lip of the English—

not all of them entirely accidental. Christian laymen are still unaware of how many changes were made in the original Bible verses in the early days of the Church, although for some years now scholars have been pointing them out to each other in books seldom seen by laymen.

It would be a shock to a literalist or "fundamentalist," for instance, to read C. S. C. Williams' *Alterations to the Text of the Synoptic Gospels and Acts* (1951), written "to show how freely the text was handled in the early days," and "the possibility of alterations for doctrinal, reverential or other reasons." In his introduction, Dr. Williams, an Oxford University Lecturer in the New Testament, points out that the scribes of the New Testament text, "whether they were orthodox or heterodox, were human; they were liable to be affected not only by carelessness but also by prejudice." And he lists a number of other scholars working on the detection of alterations, explanations, omissions, additions, harmonizations, refinements and pietistic tendencies, all of which have changed the words and meanings of the earliest manuscripts. That such changes did creep in becomes more evident every year as earlier copies of manuscripts, codices, and papyri are discovered and collated. The Dead Sea Scrolls and the Chenoboskion Gnostic codices are but the better publicized of many recent discoveries which are giving us a better idea of Jesus and his teachings, together with a number of new beatitudes attributed to him.

Before taking up the newest findings, however, we should examine briefly a group of "blessèds" which have been, so to speak, right under our noses for centuries. We have not suspected them to have been uttered by Jesus because of the poor translation of the opening words of the book they are in. They appear in the last book in the Bible, entitled (in the King James Version) The Revelation of St. John the Divine. That title is immediately contradicted in the first verse, which begins: "The Revelation of Jesus Christ, which God gave unto him. . . ." The Revised Standard Version does better in the title—The Revelation to John—but retains in the opening words: "The Revelation of Jesus Christ. . . ."

Today, "The Revelation of Jesus Christ" is most generally taken to mean the revelation about him, or his revelation of hitherto unknown facts about him. But the real meaning of the Greek, as confirmed by the context, of the first verse and the second (and, in fact, by the whole book), is that it is a revelation *by* Jesus to the author of the book, whichever John he may have been.

It is not known whether the author of the book had a number of visions or dreams in which he heard Jesus or Jesus' angel speak, or whether he is repeating sayings of Jesus which he himself had heard or which were told to him by someone else, or which he took from a collection of Agrapha or sayings of Jesus to which he had access. The last seems most probable, partly because the seven beatitudes in Revelation seem to have been rather clumsily fitted into their contexts, but more because they seem to belong in the thought patterns of Jesus as these are reflected in the Gospels:

> "Blessed is he that readeth [aloud] this scripture and those who hear it, and [especially] those that observe what is written herein, for the time is at hand" (1:3).
>
> "And I heard a voice from heaven saying, Write, Blessed are the dead that henceforth die in the Lord: Yea, saith the Spirit, that they may rest from their labors, and their works do follow them." (14:13).
>
> "Behold, I come as a thief. Blessed is he that watcheth [waketh], and keepeth his garments [on], lest he walk naked, and they see his shame" (16:15).
>
> "Blessed are they that are called unto [invited to] the marriage supper of the Lamb" (19:9).

This last beatitude refers to the Messianic Banquet the Essenes expected would take place when the Son of

Man came, and for which some scholars think Jesus'
Last Supper with his disciples was a sort of rehearsal
until "the kingdom of God shall come." All these seven
beatitudes of Revelation are apocalyptic in tone and reference. Note especially the next one: "Blessed and holy
is he who hath part in the first resurrection: on such
the second death hath no power, but they shall be priests
of God and of Christ and they shall reign with him a
thousand years" (20:6). This "thousand years" is, of
course, the millennium, which Canon R. H. Charles stated
"is first found in this book [The Secrets of Enoch],
chapter 32:2-33:2."

The sixth beatitude in Revelation is largely a review
of the first, but it is condensed and more urgent: "Behold, I come quickly: blessed is he that keepeth the sayings
of the prophecy of this book" (22:7).

The last of the seven is, "Blessed are they that do his
commandments [some manuscripts have "they that wash
their robes"] that they may have the right to the tree of
life and the right to enter the city through the gates"
(22:14). The tree of life is beautifully described in The
Secrets of Enoch as the place "where the Lord Himself
rests whenever He enters Paradise, and this tree is most
remarkable for its supremely pleasing perfume" (8:3).

The Book of Revelation records the woes, too, but
these are few and not very forceful. In 8:13 and 12:12,
they are very general ("Woe to the inhabitants of the
earth") and in the only other three (18:10, 16, 19), the
Greek word *ouai* (like the Hebrew *oy*) is for some
reason translated in the King James Version as "Alas,
alas, that great city Babylon!"

Besides the "alterations for doctrinal, reverential, or
other reasons," made by scribes, copyists and the
theology-minded Church Fathers, the pious but rather
ruthless defenders of the "faith once delivered to the
saints" even went to the extreme of burning or otherwise
destroying whole books, and the entire writings of certain scholars and schools of which they strongly disapproved and which they considered to be heretical. This

fate was meted out to two groups of books of which the orthodox theologians particularly disapproved: the entire corpus of the Enochan literature and all the "heretical" Gnostic gospels, acts and apocalypses.

In his most famous book, *Against Heresies,* Irenaeus, bishop of Lyons (A.D. 130-202), alleges that the Gnostics "adduce an unspeakable number of apocryphal and spurious writings," and that "they boast that they possess more Gospels than there really are, . . . for since there are four quarters of the world in which we live, and four universal winds, . . . it is reasonable that she [the Church] should have four pillars [i.e., the Four Gospels, Matthew, Mark, Luke, and John]. . . ."

As Dr. Adam Fyfe Findlay stated, in his interesting *Byways in Early Christian Literature* (1923): "Of all these heretical Gospels comparatively little has been preserved. The Church took care, when she gained her hard-won victory over Gnosticism, that the obnoxious writings were destroyed. When she had beaten the enemy, she burned his camp."

Until recently, about all that was known of the Gnostic literature were the quotations from it in the tracts of its orthodox Christian enemies and attackers, who were more polemical than accurate, and who were careful to quote the less admirable passages.

But in 1946, at the same time that the Qumran caves by the Dead Sea gave up many manuscripts of the Enochan literature that had escaped the attention of the Christian heresy hunters, certain Egyptian laborers, digging a trench for a foundation wall, unearthed an ancient tomb at Nag-Hammadi, near the site of ancient Chenoboskion, where Gnostic monks once flourished. In the tomb was a large urn, and in the urn was found a whole library—nearly fifty well-preserved Gnostic books, a few of which have been translated. (See my article, "Now the Gnostics," in *Library Journal,* January 1, 1960, and see also the Crest edition of my book, *The Lost Years of Jesus Revealed,* chapter 16.)

In both the Enochan literature (especially The Secrets

of Enoch) and the Gnostic books, there are beatitudes, many of them much like those of Jesus in the Gospels and Revelation.

In one of the Chenoboskion treatises, The Gospel According to Thomas, there appear eleven beatitudes and two woes attributed to Jesus himself. The Greek original is supposed to date from about A.D. 140.

Evidently, when Irenaeus and his heresy-hunters were burning every Gnostic book they could find, some clever Gnostic Christian got the bright idea of concealing in his own mortuary urn, reserved for his bones, the books he cherished most highly! (What a story, if we only knew more about him!)

Compare the following Gnostic beatitudes of Jesus from The Gospel of Thomas with the many others attributed to him:

"Jesus said, Blessed is the lion which the man eats, and the lion will become man; and cursed is the man whom the lion eats, and the man will become lion." (Figure that one out, with the help of pundits.)

"Jesus said, Blessed is he who shall stand at the beginning, for he shall know the end, and he shall not taste death." (This has to do with the doctrines of pre-existence, foreknowledge, election and resurrection.)

"Jesus said, Blessed is he who was before he became." (Here is another pre-existence one.)

"Jesus said, Blessed are the solitary and elect, for you shall find the Kingdom; for you come from it, and you shall enter into it again."

"Jesus said, Blessed are the poor, for yours is the Kingdom of Heaven." (This is practically identical with Luke 6:20.)

"Jesus said, Blessed is the man who has suffered, for he has found the Life [or "who has labored and found life"]."

"Jesus said, Blessed are you when you are hated

and persecuted: and the place where they have persecuted you will not be found." (That is, presumably, the place will be destroyed.)

"Jesus said, Blessed are those who have been persecuted in their hearts; these are they who have known the Father in truth."

"Jesus said, Blessed are the hungry, for their bellies' desires shall be filled."

"He said to her [to the woman who had said, "Blessed is the womb that bore you"], Blessed are those who have heard the word of the Father, and have kept it in truth."

"Jesus said, Blessed is the man who knows when robbers are coming, so that he will marshal his strength and gird up his loins before they arrive."

Compare also the woes:

"Jesus said, Woe to them, the Pharisees, for they are like the dog which sleeps in the manger of the oxen, for he neither eats nor lets the oxen eat."

"Jesus said, Woe to the flesh which depends upon the soul; woe to the soul that depends upon the flesh."

Many of these seem rather cryptic without a knowledge of the main "secret teachings" of the Gnostics, but then so do the Bible Gospel beatitudes without a knowledge of Christian, Jewish and Essene theology.

The beatitudes in The Secrets of Enoch—the nine beatitudes in 42:6-14, the seven beatitudes and seven woes in 52:1-14, and the scattered "isolated beatitudes" —are rather reminiscent of those already examined:

"Blessed is the man who fears the name of the Lord and serves before His face faithfully and regulates his donations by life's gifts to him: he shall live his life through to the full before he dies" (42:6).

"Blessed is the man who renders a just judgment [not for remuneration, but for justice's sake, and does not wait around for something afterward: consequently he will himself receive an impartial judgment]" (42:7).

"Blessed is he who clothes the naked with his own robe and gives his own bread to the hungry" (42:8).

"Blessed is he who secures justice for orphan and widow and gives aid to every victim of injustice" (42:9).

"Blessed is he who quits the crooked path of deceit and strides straight ahead on the right road" (42:10).

"Blessed is the sower of the seeds of righteousness, for he will harvest sevenfold" (42:11).

"Blessed is he who is so possessed of truth that he speaks the truth to his neighbor" (42:12).

"Blessed is the merciful one on whose lips are both truth and gentleness" (42:13).

"Blessed is he who recognizes the works of the Lord and glorifies Him, knowing the Craftsman by His handiwork" (42:14).

"Blessed is he who listens in his heart to praises and eulogies of the Lord" (52:1).

"Woe to him who listens in his heart to abuse and calumnies against his neighbor" (52:2).

"Blessed is he who opens his lips for blessing and glorifying the Lord" (52:3).

"Woe to him who opens his lips for cursing and blasphemy of the Lord" (52:4).

"Blessed is he who glorifies *all* the works of the Lord" (52:5).

"Woe to him who despises one of the Lord's creatures" (52:6).

"Blessed is he who considers the work of his hands to establish it" (52:7).

"Woe to him who watches in wait to wipe out the labors of others" (52:8).

"Blessed is he who preserves the institutions of the oldtime fathers" (52:9).

"Woe to him who nullifies the statutes and destroys the landmarks of his ancestors" (52:10).

"Blessed is he who goes out to seek peace and leads others to peace" (52:11).

"Woe to him who discourages the preparers of peace" (52:12).

"Blessed is he who preaches peace and is himself peaceful" (52:13).

"Woe to him who talks peace but there is no peace in his heart" (52:14).

Quoting this very chapter, Dr. A. T. Olmstead, Professor of Oriental History at the University of Chicago, states in *Jesus in the Light of History*: "Like other contemporary teachers, the author of Second Enoch for example, Jesus enunciated a series of blessings and curses." Then Dr. Olmstead quotes the beatitudes and woes of Luke 6, but he mentions no other "contemporary teacher" who gave a series of blessings and maledictions for the simple reason that no other was known. Might it have occurred to this great scholar that the anonymous author of The Secrets of Enoch, a *contemporary* of Jesus who used the same unusual literary device, could have been Jesus himself, assuming a pseudonym as did many another writer of that period?

My favorite among the isolated beatitudes is, "Blessed is he who puts confidence in men, and shows it by bringing help to the condemned, and soothing the bruised, and doing a favor when asked; for on the Great Judgment Day every deed of man will be revealed in writing. Blessed is he whose measure and weight and balances will then be found true, because at the Great Judgment Day all measures, weights and balances will be exposed to view as in the market-place; and everyone will recognize his own measure, and according to *that* measure he will be paid" (44:4-5).

Compare this with the one that appears, with slight

variations, in all three Synoptic Gospels (Matthew 7:2, Mark 4:24 and Luke 6:38): "Give, and it shall be given unto you, good measure, for with what measure ye mete, it shall be measured to you again." (In Luke it appears as "with the same measure that ye mete withal it shall be measured to you again.")

One more of these isolated beatitudes in The Secrets of Enoch (48:9) has a connection with the better-known sayings of Jesus. After Enoch records what he has seen in the seven heavens and what the Lord has told him, he is sent back to earth to deliver the books to his children, "and they to their children, parents to parents, generation by generation" (33:9). "Then, in the later history of that race, will come to light the books written by your hand and by your father's, when the angel-guardians of the earth will show them to men of faith, . . . and the books will be praised thereafter more than at first" (35:2,3). This seems somewhat prophetic —or a bit weird, anyway—for the book was written between A.D. 1 and 50, and nineteen centuries later parts of at least ten Enochan books have "come to light" in caves beside the Salty Sea! But, of course, as all great scholars will be quick to admit, it is mere coincidence.

Enoch does get back to earth. After he tells of his experiences and of the wonders he has seen in the seven heavens—the stables of the clouds, the heavy chains of the thunder, and how the stars "flash forth like fire in indescribable beauty," Enoch, always the leisurely narrator, finally says to his children: "Take these books, written by your own father's hand, and read them, and from them learn the works of the Lord. There have been plenty of books since the beginning of creation, and there will be many until the consummation of the age, but none of them will reveal things to you like my manuscript" (47:2,3).

After this excellent "commercial" (which is vaguely reminiscent of the many new and competitive versions and revisions of the Bible), Enoch says: "Now distribute these books to your children and children's children, to all your relatives, and to all people of intelligence. Those who have wisdom, and fear the Lord, will welcome these books as more pleasing than the finest food, and will read them and become attached to them; whereas the unintelligent persons who do not even know about the Lord will not accept these books, but will push them aside, for their yoke would lie heavy on them" (48:6-9).

Now consider the enigmatic but important isolated beatitude which appears in 48:9: "Blessed is he who puts on their yoke and works faithfully in it, for he will be acquitted on the Great Judgment Day." In other words, Enoch is saying that many men will find it burdensome to live up to the standard of morality and helpfulness set in the beatitudes, and to obey the other admonitions recorded in the heavens at the dictation of the Lord and his angels. Many men will reject that "yoke" as too heavy. Nevertheless, those who do accept the books and follow the advice given in them will find at the Day of Judgment that they will easily pass the examination and be acquitted and released. Long before that, once they have "put on their yoke" (i.e., read and accepted these books of Enoch), they will find the books "more pleasing than the finest food," and will cling to the "yoke" and love it.

The writer of The Secrets of Enoch is rather familiar with this image of the yoke. In one chapter, the Lord, predicting the forthcoming Deluge and telling the reasons for it, says, "I know the wickedness of men, that they will not endure the weight of the yoke that I shall lay upon them, nor sow the seed I have given them; but will throw off My yoke and take another yoke, and sow unsound seed [beget worthless offspring], who will worship false gods and reject My sovereignty" (34:1).

These references to yokes and their relative weights, written by a contemporary of Jesus, provide a fuller comprehension of the thought patterns and imagery already familiar to Jesus and his hearers when he said, "Come unto me, all ye that labor and are heavy laden, and I will give you rest. Take my yoke upon you, and learn of me; for I am meek and lowly in heart: and ye shall find rest unto your souls. For my yoke is easy, and my burden is light" (Matthew 11:28-30).

Because so much in The Secrets of Enoch parallels or is later expanded in the beatitudes of Jesus as given in the canonical Gospels, there is justification in raising the question of the identity of this anonymous author, for the beatitudes were not only characteristic of Jesus: they were the very core of his teaching.

I became aware of and impressed with the fact that the Matthean beatitudes are the epitome of the Gospel messages and beliefs of Jesus, when, in my late teens, I read Adolf Harnack's brilliant essay, *Das Wesen des Christenthums* ("The Essence of Christianity"): "Should we be threatened with doubts as to what He [Jesus] meant, we must steep ourselves again and again in the Beatitudes of the Sermon on the Mount. They contain His ethics and His religion, united at the roots. . . ."

Of course there are a number of "blesseds" in the Old Testament, particularly in the Psalms, but they are, for the most part, mere exclamations—usually consisting of one simple phrase, such as "Blessed be the Lord God of Israel," or "Blessed be all they that fear God."

Jesus took these pious, often mystical, vague and ecstatic expressions of praise and loyalty and built them into a powerful, condensed literary and sermonic form— each sentence a homily in itself, easily remembered because brief and pungent.

Always the finished beatitude, the polished *macarism*, can be recognized by its structure: two phrases or clauses, the first of which states the desirable virtue or condition to be achieved or the service to be rendered, while the second promises the blessedness or reward which will result. There are infinite variations—sometimes the second clause is placed first—but a genuine beatitude, evolved and uttered by Jesus, is easily recognized.

So, to sum up this study of the beatitudes as related to both canonical and noncanonical writings, and discarding the traditional but unverified assumption that Jesus never wrote any scripture, is it not reasonable to assume that an anonymous book, written during his lifetime, and containing two sets of the beatitudes (his favorite form of expression when teaching), may possibly have been written by him—particularly since two of his Gospel biographers quote similar sets of his beatitudes? This supposition is strengthened by recent discoveries of similar beatitudes attributed to him by ancient non-canonical witnesses.

If this theory is correct—if Jesus did write The Secrets of Enoch or part of it before beginning his public teaching and while he was formulating (perhaps at Qumran) his philosophy of life and his religious message—then the beatitudes in that book should be expected to foreshadow those he later pronounced to his disciples. Some of the Enochan beatitudes might be more or less experimental and somewhat immature, but would have in them traces of the more developed and perfected forms given later. That is exactly what we do find, although personally I prefer several of the Enochan beatitudes to some of the canonical ones, at least in the form in which the latter have reached us.

But no one who compares the Enochan beatitudes with those in Matthew, Luke or Revelation, or in the recently discovered Gospel of Thomas, can fail to recognize their relationship, nor can he refuse to admit the possibility that many of them were the work of one man.

CHAPTER 7

Ethics of Enoch and Jesus

The day-by-day teachings of Jesus are recorded almost entirely in his own words in the canonical Gospels (639 verses in Matthew, 333 in Mark, 580 in Luke and 419 in John), but in the red-letter New Testaments, he is also allotted twenty-seven verses in the Acts, two in First Corinthians, one in Second Corinthians and sixty-two in Revelation. Why didn't the editors of these Testaments include the seven beatitudes of Revelation (1:3, 14:13, 16:15, 19:9, 20:6, 22:7 and 22:14)? In his article on beatitudes in Hastings' *Dictionary of the Bible,* the renowned Greek New Testament scholar, Dr. J. H. Moulton, states: "There is no guarantee that even Matthew gives all the beatitudes pronounced by Jesus on different occasions. . . . It is at least possible that in other parts of the New Testament we have quotations from sayings of the same kind. Thus First Peter 4:14, James 1:12, Revelation 14:13 might easily be supposed to rest on words of Christ."

To these might be added, with equal reason, First

78

Peter 3:14 and James 1:25. And since Dr. Moulton mentions Revelation 14:13, one of the seven beatitudes in Revelation (which we have already attributed to Jesus as probable author), why does he not include the other six? He admits, in this same article, that "all attempts to ascertain the original form of sayings of Jesus have at best so large a subjective element that we cannot afford to dogmatize . . . so that elements not included in the principal Gospel sources may nevertheless be derived from firsthand authority."

That honest, open-minded statement clearly affords a basis for including the best and most apparently veridical of the noncanonical "Sayings of Jesus" in this appraisal, especially the aphorisms and precepts in The Secrets of Enoch as they are compared with the teachings of Jesus as given in the canonical New Testament scriptures.

The latter can be roughly divided into two groups: those which give advice about conduct or human relations, and those which deal with the future, or eschatology—such "last things" as death, resurrection, immortality, the end of the world, the Last Judgment, heaven, hell and eternity.

Here we shall compare Jesus' teachings on conduct or human relations, as recorded in the New Testament, with those of the pseudonymous author of The Secrets of Enoch.

Of course, it is impossible to separate completely tenets of conduct from theories and beliefs about the future. What theologians have called *interims ethik,* the "temporary ethic" which necessarily determines one's conduct when he believes the end of the world is imminent, is much different from the ethics of a man who expects the earth to keep on pursuing its orbit round the sun. If Jesus believed that the end of the world would come in his generation, are his ethical teachings valid and normative today? That is the question perennially confronting Christianity. Various answers have been offered, but none has been very satisfactory.

Jesus' teachings about conduct (or "human relations," as it is often referred to nowadays) may be divided into ten specific subjects in order to sharpen and focalize ideas which might otherwise seem nebulous. We shall consider in turn what Jesus and the author of The Secrets of Enoch had to say about charity and benevolence; honesty, righteousness and justice; purity of heart or motive; peace and pacifism; patience in enduring affliction; exalted view of man; anger and murder; love toward others, or the Golden Rule; humility; and kindness to animals. (It is interesting to note that this ethic derives from Zoroaster's teachings.)

To facilitate this comparison, the New Testament teachings of Jesus and the advice given by the author of The Secrets of Enoch will be shown in parallel columns. This will not be an exhaustive or exhausting argumentative study: just enough excerpts will be included to show the similarity between the two books.

But we are concerned here not so much with the similarities of language and vocabulary as with similarity of ideas and doctrines, even though these may be expressed in quite different words and phrases.

Charity and Benevolence

Secrets of Enoch

9:1: ". . . This place [Paradise], Enoch, is prepared for the righteous who . . . give bread to the hungry, cover with their own robe the naked, lift up the fallen, help the wronged, and walk blameless in the sight of the Lord."

42:8: "Blessed is he who with his own robe clothes the naked and gives his own bread to the hungry."

New Testament

Matthew 25:34-40: "Then shall the King say unto them on his right hand, Come ye blessed of my Father, inherit the kingdom prepared for you from the foundation of the world: For I was an hungered, and ye gave me meat: I was thirsty and ye gave me drink: I was a stranger, and ye took me in: Naked, and ye clothed me: I was sick and ye visited me: I was in

44:4: "Blessed is he who puts confidence in man, and shows it by bringing help to the condemned, and soothing the bruised and doing a favor when asked." [One version has the last phrase, "giving generously to the needy."]

50:5: "Lose your gold and your silver for your brother's sake."

51:1,2: "Extend your hands to the orphan and the widow, and according to your ability help the destitute, and they will prove to be like a shelter in the time of storm."

[See also 63:1.]

prison, and ye came unto me. Then shall the righteous answer him, saying, Lord, when saw we thee an hungered, and fed thee? or thirsty, and gave thee drink? . . . And the King shall answer, . . . Verily I say unto you, Inasmuch as ye have done it unto one of the least of these my brethren, ye have done it unto me."

Mark 10:21: "Then Jesus beholding him [the rich young ruler], loved him and said, One thing thou lackest: go thy way, sell whatever thou hast, and give to the poor, and thou shalt have treasure in heaven. . . ."

[See also Matthew 5:42, 6:1-4, 11:2-5, Luke 3:11, 6:30-38, 10:33-35, 11:41, 12:33, 14:12-14, 19:8-9, and Acts of the Apostles 20:35, where Paul quotes Jesus saying, "It is more blessed to give than to receive."]

Honesty, Righteousness and Justice

Secrets of Enoch
42:7: "Blessed is the man

New Testament
Matthew 5:6: "Blessed are

who renders a just judgment."

42:10: "Blessed is he who quits the crooked path of deceit and strides straight ahead on the right road."

42:11: "Blessed is the sower of the seeds of righteousness, for he will harvest sevenfold."

42:12: "Blessed is he who is so possessed of truth that he speaks the truth to his neighbor."

44:5 [condensed]: "Blessed is he whose measure and weight and balances will be found true [when exposed to view at the Great Judgment Day]."

46:3: "For when the Lord sends His great Light . . . there will be one righteous judgment, without respect of persons, for the just and the unjust; no man there will remain concealed."

[See also 42:9, 46:2, 49:1 and 52:16.]

they who do hunger and thirst after righteousness: for they shall be filled."

Matthew 5:20: "For I say unto you, That except your righteousness shall exceed the righteousness of the scribes and Pharisees, ye shall in no case enter into the kingdom of heaven."

John 3:20,21: "For every one that doeth evil hateth the light, neither cometh to the light, lest his deeds should be discovered. But he that doeth truth cometh to the light, that his deeds may be made manifest, that they are wrought in God."

John 7:24: "Judge not according to the appearance, but judge righteous judgment."

John 16:8-13: "And when he [the Comforter] is come, he will convince the world regarding sin, and righteousness and judgment. . . . I have yet many things to say unto you, but ye cannot bear them now. Howbeit when he, the Spirit of truth, is come, he will guide you into all truth. . . ."

[See also Matthew 5:10, 7:1-5, 25:41-46; Mark 4: 24; Luke 6:37-38.]

Purity of Heart or Motive

Secrets of Enoch

45:3: "Is it that the Lord has need of offerings of bread or candles or sheep or cattle? (These are nothing: He desires a pure heart.) But with these He tests the heart of man."

52:16: "Meanwhile then, my children, keep your hearts [pure] from all evil: so that when you are weighed in the balances in the bright light of Judgment Day, you will not need to hide, but will shine resplendent among the children of light forever."

[See also 46:1-2, 52:1-2, [61:4-5.]

New Testament

Matthew 5:8: "Blessed are the pure in heart: for they shall see God."

Matthew 12:34-35: "O generation of vipers, how can ye, being evil, speak good things? for out of the abundance of the heart the mouth speaketh. A good man out of the good treasure of the heart bringeth forth good things: and an evil man out of the evil treasure bringeth forth evil things."

[See also Matthew 13:15, 15:8; Luke 1:66, 8:15; John 14:1.]

Peace and Pacifism

Secrets of Enoch

50:2-3: "Now then, my children, dwell in patience and peace the rest of your allotted days, that you may inherit the eternal age to come. . . ."

52:11-14: "Blessed is he who makes peace. Woe to him who discourages the peacemakers. Blessed is he

New Testament

Matthew 5:9: "Blessed are the peacemakers: for they shall be called the children of God."

John 14:27: "Peace I leave with you, my peace I give unto you: not as the world giveth, give I unto you. Let not your heart be troubled, neither let it be afraid."

who preaches peace and is himself peaceful. Woe to him who talks peace but there is no peace in his heart."

54:1: "Explain my books to all who ask, that they may be for you a heritage of peace."

66:6: "Even in the distress of your tribulations, walk in patience and peace [or humility] until you depart from this world of suffering [that you may become heirs of eternity]."

[See also 19:3 and especially 33:1-2: ". . . at the end of seven thousand years, . . . a millennium of rest and peace, when years will end. . . ."]

John 16:33: "These things have I spoken unto you, that in me ye might have peace. In the world ye shall have tribulation: but be of good cheer: I have overcome the world."

[See also John 20:19,21.]

Patience in Enduring Affliction

Secrets of Enoch
9:1: "And the two men replied, This place [Paradise], Enoch, is prepared for the righteous who, in their lifetime, endure troubles which distress their souls; yet they avoid iniquity, . . . and walk blameless in the sight of the Lord. It is for these that this place is prepared for an everlasting inheritance."

New Testament
Matthew 5:10-12: "Blessed are they who are persecuted for righteousness sake: for theirs is the kingdom of heaven. Blessed are ye when men shall revile you, and persecute you, and shall say all manner of evil against you falsely, for my sake. Rejoice and be exceeding glad: for so persecuted they

51:3: "Every distressing and heavy yoke, if it is thrust on you on account of the Lord, cast it off, and thereby you will meet with your reward on the Day of Judgment." [This appears in the oldest and best manuscripts, *U* and *M*, but others have: ". . . thrust on you, endure all for the Lord's sake, and so you will receive your reward."]

62:1: "Blessed is the man who in patience carries his gift before the Lord, for he will receive his reward." [The context shows that "in patience" means "without murmuring."]

66:6: "Even in the distress of your tribulations, walk in patience and humility until you depart from this world of suffering. . . ."

[See also 55:2,3 and 65:8-10.]

the prophets which were before you."

Matthew 10:22: "And ye shall be hated of all men for my name's sake: but he that endureth to the end shall be saved."

Luke 6:22,23: "Blessed are ye when men shall hate you, and when they shall separate you from their company, and shall reproach you, and cast out your name as evil, for the Son of Man's sake. Rejoice ye in that day, and leap for joy: for, behold, your reward is great in heaven. . . ."

Luke 8:15: "But that [seed which fell] on the good ground are they which in an honest and good heart, having heard the word, keep it, and bring forth fruit with patience."

Luke 21:17-19: "And ye shall be hated of all men for my name's sake. But there shall not an hair of your head perish. In your patience possess ye your souls."

[See also Mark 13:13 and Revelation 2.]

Exalted View of Man

Secrets of Enoch

44:1-5: "With his own hands the Lord created man in the likeness of His own countenance: small or great, the Lord made him. Whoever insults the face of man insults the Lord's face . . . but the wrath of the Lord in the Great Judgment will consume him who spits in the face of a man. . . . Blessed is he who puts confidence in man, and shows it by . . . giving generously to the needy. . . ."

52:2,3: "The Lord summoned all the wild and domestic animals of the earth and all the living birds, and brought them before our father Adam . . . and for complete submission and obedience to man. For the Lord created man to be the steward of all his possessions."

60:1: "Whoever does injury to the soul of man does wrong to his own soul, and there is no healing for him forever."

[Chapter 30 is largely in praise of man: I quote brief passages. The Lord is

New Testament

Matthew 5:44-48: ". . . Love your enemies, bless them that curse you, do good to them that hate you. . . . That ye may be the children of your Father . . . for he maketh his sun to rise on the evil and on the good, and sendeth rain on the just and on the unjust. . . . Be ye therefore perfect, even as your Father which is in heaven is perfect."

Matthew 12:12, 12:8: "How much then is a man better than a sheep! Wherefore it is lawful to do well on the sabbath days [by healing the sick]. For the Son of Man is Lord even of the sabbath day."

[To call attention to his exalted view of man, Jesus constantly emphasized the fact that he was a man himself, although doing what seemed greater things than a mere man could do. Eighty times he is quoted as referring to himself as the Son of Man.]

John 5:24-27: "Verily, verily, I say unto you, He that heareth my word, and bespeaking to Enoch in the seventh heaven. (This is only in the longer [later] recension.)]

30:10: ". . . I contrived to make man of a nature which was at the same time material and spiritual, of both death and life, and although resembling in appearance any other creation . . . , yet he alone knows speech. And on the earth I set him like a second angel, noble, great, and glorious. I established him as King of the Earth, having the Kingdom by My Wisdom. . . . And I gave him his free will, and I showed him the two roads, the Road of Light and the Road of Darkness, and I said to him: This one is good and that one is evil . . ."

lieveth on him that sent me, hath everlasting life, . . . [and] is passed from death unto life. . . . The hour is coming, and now is, when the dead shall hear the voice of the Son of God: and they that hear shall live. For the Father . . . hath given to the Son to have life in himself: And hath given him authority . . . because he is the Son of Man."

[And in John 14:12 he stressed the fact that his disciples could do the things he did if they only believed: "He that believeth on me, the works that I do shall he do also; and greater works than these shall he do; because I go unto my Father."

John 1:12: "But as many as received him, to them gave he power to become the sons of God, even to them that believe on his name."

Anger and Murder

Secrets of Enoch
60:2-4: "He who commits a murder kills his own soul, and there is no healing for him forever. He who drives a man into a net will be caught in it himself, and he

New Testament
Matthew 5:21: "Ye have heard that it was said to them of old time, Thou shalt not commit murder; and whosoever shall commit murder shall be in danger

who drives a man into court will not escape his own judgment in Eternity."

[See also 44:1-3.]

of the judgment: But I say unto you that whosoever is angry with his brother without a cause shall be in danger of the judgment. . . ."

Love Toward Others (Golden Rule)

Secrets of Enoch

42:13: "Blessed is he on whose lips are both truth and gentleness."

46:2: "Or if one man deludes another by a lie, having good on his tongue but evil in his heart, does he not know it himself, and know that he will be condemned, since his untruthfulness will be revealed to all . . . when the Lord sends His great Light. . . ."

50:5: "Lose [spend] your gold and your silver for your brother's sake, and you will receive ample treasure (not of the carnal kind) on the Day of Judgment."

60:1: "Whoever does injury to the soul of man does wrong to his own soul. . . ."

61: "Now then, my children, . . . abstain from any prejudice against any living soul which the Lord has created. That which a man

New Testament

Matthew 5:43-47: "Ye have heard that it hath been said, Thou shalt love thy neighbor and hate thine enemy. But I say unto you, Love your enemies. . . . For if ye love them which love you, . . . and if ye salute your brethren only, what do ye more than others? do not even the publicans so?"

Matthew 19:19: "Thou shalt love thy neighbor as thyself."

Luke 12:33, 34: "Sell that ye have, and give alms; provide yourselves bags which wax not old, a treasure in the heavens that faileth not, where no thief approacheth, neither moth corrupteth. For where your treasure is, there will your heart be also."

John 13:34, 35: "A new commandment I give unto you, That ye love one another; as I have loved you, asks from the Lord for his own soul, let him pray that He do it likewise for every living soul."

that ye also love one another. By this shall all men know that ye are my disciples if ye have love one to another."

John 15:9-17 (especially verse 13): "Greater love hath no man than this, that a man lay down his life for his friends."

Humility

Secrets of Enoch

[In the second heaven Enoch encounters condemned angels dismally weeping who ask him to pray for them.]
7:5: ". . . Who am I, a mere mortal, to intercede for angels! . . . And who, indeed, is going to pray for *me*?"

63:1-4: "A man who covers the naked and to the hungering gives bread will be recompensed [in the Great Age]; but if his heart murmurs, then the charity is spoiled, and he will not receive any reward. And if he overfeeds the needy, and becomes proud and scornful in his alms-giving, then he nullifies all his good works and gains nothing,

New Testament

Matthew 5:3,5: "Blessed are the poor in spirit: for theirs is the kingdom of heaven. Blessed are the meek: for they shall inherit the earth."

Matthew 11:29: "Take my yoke upon you and learn of me; for I am meek and lowly in heart: and ye shall find rest unto your souls."

Matthew 18:4: "Whosoever therefore shall humble himself as this little child, the same is greatest in the kingdom of heaven."

Matthew 23:12: "And whosoever shall exalt himself shall be abased; and he that shall humble himself shall be exalted."

Mark 10:43-44: ". . . who-for the Lord abominates every arrogant man."

66:6: ". . . walk in patience and peace until you depart from this world of suffering. . . ."

soever will be great among you should be your servant: And whosoever would be greatest should be willing to be the slave of all."

Luke 14:8: "When thou art bidden . . . to a wedding, sit not down in the highest place. . . . But . . . sit down in the lowest seat, so that then he that bade thee cometh, he may say unto thee, Friend, go up higher. . . ."

[See also Matthew 20:26; Mark 9:33; Luke 6:20, 9:46-48, 22:24-27; John [13:4,5,14,15.]

Kindness to Animals

Secrets of Enoch

58:2-6: "The Lord summoned all the wild and domestic animals of the earth, and all the living birds and brought them before our father Adam, that he might give names to all living things on the earth. . . . He made them all mute, for complete submission and obedience to man. For the Lord created man to be the steward of all His possessions. Therefore there will be no judgment of every living soul, but of man

New Testament

Matthew 6:26: "Behold the fowls of the air: for they sow not, neither do they reap, nor gather into barns; yet your heavenly Father feedeth them." [Luke 12:4 specifies "ravens."]

Matthew 10:29: "Are not two sparrows sold for a farthing? and one of them shall not fall on the ground without your Father." [Luke 12:6 has ". . . not one of them is forgotten before God."]

alone. For in the Great Age there will be one place, one fold, one pasture, for all the souls of animals. For the case will not be closed for one animal soul . . . until the Judgment. But all animal souls will accuse man at the Judgment if poorly fed."

59:1,5: "Whoever feeds poorly the soul of animals is unfair to his own soul. . . . Whoever does harm to an animal in secret, that is a bad custom; it is a defilement of his own soul."

Luke 14:5: ". . . Which of you shall have an ass or an ox fallen into a pit, and will not straightway pull him out [even] on the sabbath day?" [Matthew 12:11 has "a sheep."]

[Jesus seemed to like doves: he told his disciples (Matthew 10:16) to be wise as serpents but harmless as doves. He drove the sellers of doves out of the temple (Matthew 21:12). And the dove which settled on his head at his baptism may have recognized him as an old friend, and have come for more of the usual crumbs. All four Gospel writers mention the dove descending upon him (Matthew 3:16, Mark 1:10, Luke 3:22 and John 1:32), however much they disagree on details.]

CHAPTER 8

The Virgin Birth* and Melchizedek

The study of The Secrets of Enoch, which began some forty years ago, has not yet been able to account for the fact that the miraculous birth of Melchizedek was substituted for Noah's nativity in First Enoch. When a pseudepigrapher quoted or copied any earlier work, he took whatever liberties he wished. Had this deviation any particular significance?

If the scribe was connected with the Essenes, he might have made the change for a creedal reason. Melch-Zadok (as the name was written in Hebrew) was to the Essenes the King of Righteousness, and they called themselves the Sons of Zadok, who was God's own chosen "priest of priests forever" (Second Enoch, 71:29). So, Melchizedek was revered as a saint by that pious sect.

---

* Taking the negative side of "Resolved, That the Miraculous Virgin Birth of Jesus Christ Is a Fact and That It Is an Essential Christian Doctrine," the author won the debate from the famous New York City clergyman, John Roach Straton, at Carnegie Hall, March 22, 1924. [Eds.]

Another possible factor is that, in the Epistle to the Hebrews, Jesus was "made a high priest forever after the order of Melchizedek" (6:20), and Melchizedek is described as born "without father, without mother, without descent, having neither beginning of days, nor end of life" (7:3). In other words, he was the direct creation of Yahweh.

This is beyond human comprehension, nor does it explain the riddle of the different birth narratives in the two Enochs. Why was the Melchizedek story expunged from several pseudepigraphic manuscripts after being included (doubtless copied from The Secrets of Enoch before its loss) in the Book of Jubilees?

Had this "editing" been ordered by the Hebrew hierarchy in an effort to keep the fabulous tale from the public? If so, for what reason? Supernatural acts and events were common enough in the Old Testament, and cause for pride. But in neither book in which Melchizedek is mentioned, Genesis nor Psalms, was anything said of his birth, miraculous or otherwise. Elders and rabbis knew it to be an invention of the pseudepigraphic school (which arrogated to itself too much omniscience) and strove to check it lest simple folk be led astray. A death penalty had been set on anonymous authors who hid behind great names and published insidious scriptural works.

But why was a small segment which was not at all heretical or politically dangerous selected for obliteration? The violent ripping out of this section from the admired Book of Jubilees seems far too emotional to be attributed to cold official censorship. To question this act, after a lapse of nineteen centuries, may sound ridiculous, but I do.

Again and again, I returned to the ancient riddle which apparently bothered nobody else. Suddenly, there occurred to me a provocative solution: Perhaps the deletion of Melchizedek's miraculous birth had a bearing on the Virgin Birth of Jesus, belief in which spread after his crucifixion, as proof that he was the Messiah. Also, word may have reached the affronted religious leaders that the executed criminal had been the writer of The Secrets of Enoch, which exploited the nativity of Melchizedek for his own false purposes! Orthodox Jewry could not tolerate such heresy, and the children of Israel must be protected from this religious quackery.

This thought led me to think of the familiar, much-discussed fact of the meager consideration given the Virgin Birth in the Gospels and elsewhere in the New Testament, despite its vital importance to Christian doctrine. Whatever else is doubted or banned, two things must remain in the Faith: the supernatural birth and the bodily resurrection. On the former depends the sinlessness of Jesus; on the latter, the certainty of the general resurrection of the dead.

The very idea of a virgin mother was objectionable to the Jews. This is felt in the undertone of the first two chapters of Matthew, in the writer's efforts to placate existing prejudices and to answer the arguments of his readers. He appealed to the national pride of his race by providing the genealogical table of Jesus, which traces his lineage to King David, from whose line the Messiah was to spring. Matthew drew on other scriptural citations that "it might be fulfilled." Of course, the crowning reference was to the awesome prophet Isaiah's prediction of the virginal birth of God's Anointed: "Behold, a virgin shall conceive and bear a son" (7:14). (Modern biblical scholars point out that Isaiah used the Hebrew word *almah,* signifying a young woman of marriageable age, instead of the word *bethula,* which connotes a virgin.)

Matthew's Gospel does not mention the Virgin Birth and it is supported only by Luke, who varies the details considerably, as though he had drawn them from different sources or oral tradition.

The earliest of the Gospels (written about A.D. 65), that according to Mark, makes no mention of the Virgin Birth, or of Jesus' life before his baptism by John the Baptist and the beginning of his fateful ministry. This omission is laid to the fact that Mark got most of his data from Peter, with whom he went on preaching tours (see the Book of Acts). Peter was noted for citing only those facts of which he had firsthand knowledge, and for not being likely to vouch for anything he hadn't witnessed. This, together with the fact that the Virgin Birth had never been brought up in early apostolic preaching, is the explanation given for Mark's silence.

Luke, however, provides a poetic and dramatic elaboration of the circumstances of Jesus' birth, although he does not emphasize the actual event (except for the angelic witnesses from the skies and the amazed shepherds). Luke's unique and beautiful description of the Annunciation and of the subsequent meetings of Mary and Elizabeth is his version of Divine transcendence into earthly life. It must be added, however, that the heavenly dialogue between Gabriel and Mary, which heralds the Virgin Birth (Luke 1:34-35) is held by some highly esteemed exegetes to be an interpolation in the text. Also, it has been authoritatively noted that Luke's narrative of the nativity is given from Mary's viewpoint, and certain social-life conclusions drawn as to derivation; in Matthew, the narrative is given entirely from Joseph's side. But the two Evangelists supplement each other's accounts of the nativity scene: one describes the manger, the angelic chorus and the shepherds; the other, the Star leading the Wise Men of the East to Bethlehem.

None of this physical description is to be found in the Fourth Gospel. But certain passages in John's prologue to his profoundly mystical interpretation of Jesus have, since the days of the Church Fathers, been considered to refer to the miracle of the conception. Witness: ". . . born not of the blood, nor of the will of the flesh, but of God" and "the Word became flesh, and dwelt among us and we beheld his glory" (John 1:13-14).

It has been reasonably deduced that John did not care to go beyond this mystical mode of expression, for during the time of his authorship a controversy raged over the reality of the Incarnation, which involved belief in the Virgin Birth. Whether or not this controversy affected his attitude, the Roman Creed, as far back as A.D. 100 adopted the doctrine in the words " . . . who was born of the Holy Ghost from the Virgin Mary."

Outside the growing membership of the new faith, this idea was received with astonishment. The Jews had never regarded virginity as a state superior to that of marriage. Indeed, cohabitation before marriage—though looked upon as reprehensible—was not regarded as a reason for forbidding the union. The Gentile world was very perplexed about the solemnization of the doctrine of the Virgin Birth. A second-century Greek, Aristides, sought to explain the doctrine in a letter to the Emperor Antoninus Pius:

> "The Christians, then, reckon the beginning of their religion from Jesus the Messiah, and he is named the Son of God Most High; and it is said that God came down from heaven, and from a Hebrew virgin took and clothed himself with flesh, and in a daughter of man dwelt the Son of God."

Emperor Antoninus Pius probably knit his brows in ever greater puzzlement and left the problem to his successor, Marcus Aurelius, to solve (he didn't, except by persecuting the Christians severely during his reign).

The Apostle Paul, some of whose Epistles (A.D. 62-67) even preceded the Gospel of Mark in general circulation, never employed the dogma of the Virgin Birth in his missionary work among the Gentiles. This is surprising, for the Greeks and Romans traditionally believed that extraordinary individuals had an extraordinary origin. But Paul disregarded this excellent inducement to use the Virgin Birth, and preached instead what seems contrary persuasion. Jesus was "made of the seed of David according to the flesh" and was the Son of God "by the resurrection from the dead" (Romans 1:3-4).

Paul was not alone in making no mention of the miraculous entrance into life of this supreme person. Nowhere in the New Testament is belief in Jesus Christ made dependent on the Virgin Birth. Jesus himself never refers to it nor even suggests it in the biographical Gospels. Neither Mary nor Joseph show any consciousness of their first son's supernatural origin. But their reticence can be understood in the incredible circumstances. In all probability, it was a closely guarded family secret, which became known only gradually. So, for excellent reasons, Mary "kept all these things and pondered them in her heart," until, as has been conjectured by scholarly exegesis, Mary confessed to a woman confidant—if not to Luke himself—the wonders of Jesus' birth. Theory, of course, but the feminine influence in the beauty and delicacy of that portion of the Third Gospel is undeniable.

The calumny that followed the establishment of the claim of the Virgin Birth was full proof of the wisdom of withholding it from the public as long as possible. At once the hasty marriage of Joseph and Mary—he an old man, Mary a girl—assumed suspicious overtones. It was simply in their human nature for the couple's neighbors and observers, especially the women, to invent a lover and a clandestine romance. Joseph was highly respected, but they must have added sagely: "There's no fool like an old fool."

Such rumors multiplied and spread until they reached the ears of the authorities, who—for polemical purposes and because of their hatred of Christians—found the alleged illegitimacy of Jesus a most effective weapon to use against the new religion and its adherents. In the early rabbinical literature, the Mishna refers to Jesus as a *mamzer* ("bastard").

Pseudepigraphic writers took up the theme. One, in his Gospel of Nicodemus, asserted that Jesus "was born of fornication" between his parents before their marriage. The Talmud identified Mary as Miriam, an adulterous hairdresser. One talmudic writer has Mary admit the illegitimacy of her son to the famous Rabbi Akiba.

On the other hand, the anonymous Gospel of James, believed to have been written in the second century A.D., defends to the last the divinity of Jesus Christ against all Jewish vilifiers and against those apologetic Christians who sought to excuse his lowly heritage. Wasn't the hallowed Moses an abandoned infant found among the reeds? And weren't most of the prophets born of poor people?

The wordy battle continued into the Middle Ages, the crowning infamy being the *Toledoth Jeshu,* in which the worst versions of the life of Jesus were gathered together in venomous company, to widen the breach between Jew and Christian. Of course, the Christian retaliated with defamation and persecution.

To combat their foes, early supporters of the Virgin Birth set about inventing apocryphal stories of Jesus' childhood. Except for the striking incident of how his father and mother, worried at his three-day absence, discovered the twelve-year-old Jesus in deep discussion with wise elders in the Jerusalem Temple, there had been no other report of childhood exploits. Why, he was a prodigy, and couldn't help doing marvelous things! They, the imaginative pseudepigraphers, would provide them, and help the boy to fame. He could be another Samuel, beloved of Yahweh.

What they wrote was extremely naive and foolish at best, but it followed the popular pattern of current Jewish literature, which provided pious entertainment and instruction (much like the mid-nineteenth century Maria Edgeworth stories for Sabbath reading).

In one such work of the second or third century, entitled *Pseudo-Matthew,* there is a scene in which fearful dragons come out of a cave to worship the child Jesus. An escort of fierce wild beasts voluntarily accompanies the Holy Family on its flight into Egypt, where the marvelous boy learns the arts of sorcery. On his return to Nazareth, the young magician uses this secret knowledge to awe his neighbors and playmates. A typical instance is in the Arabic Gospel of the Infancy of Jesus Christ, quoted in full to illustrate the lighter side of apocalyptic imagination:

"Another day the Lord Jesus went out into the street, and seeing some boys who had set to play, he followed them; but the boys hid themselves from him. Therefore when the Lord Jesus had come to the door of a certain house and saw the women who stood there, he asked them whither the boys had gone. And when they told him that there was nobody there, the Lord Jesus said again: What are these that ye see in the vault? They answered that they were kids of three years old. Then the Lord Jesus cried aloud and said: Come out here, O kids, to your shepherd! The boys came out, having the form of kids, and began to skip about him.

"When they saw it the women wondered greatly, and being seized with fear, they suppliantly and in haste adored Lord Jesus, saying: O our Lord Jesus, Son of Mary, thou art indeed the good shepherd of Israel; have pity on thy handmaids who stand before thee and never doubted; for O our Lord, thou hast come to heal and not to destroy . . . but now we pray thee, and from thy kindness, we ask that thou wouldst restore these boys thy servants to their former condition. The Lord Jesus therefore said: Come out, boys, let us go and play. And immediately, while the women stood there, the kids were changed into boys."

But let us leave fancy for fact. Scientists have verified that third sets of teeth and renewed eyesight occur at times in the aged, but virginal conception of human life by humans is unknown. This remarkable process, called parthenogenesis, is found in lice, caddis flies, silkworms, maggots and various genera of beetles. There is no record of parthenogenesis in the higher forms of life. That it cannot happen, however, no one who believes in the omnipotence of the Almighty will assert. Nor is it certain that science, already busy on the problem, will not one day discover in the laboratory the secret of the creation of life.

Births beyond nature have been a familiar idea to many peoples. Ancient people believed that a passing contact with a god or a divine glance was enough to waken life in the womb of a woman. Often, impregnation came by way of a dream or a magical substance. Fo-hi, the legendary founder of the Chinese Empire, was the son of a virgin, who conceived by eating a strange flower that clung to her garment. Before Buddha was born, his mother, who was a pure and honest wife, dreamed that a six-headed white elephant entered her side. Pundits interpreted this as the conception of the Enlightened One, who wished to be reborn to teach mankind the blessings of nirvana. Egypt, too, claimed a miraculous birth: Amenhotep III, the Eighteenth Dynasty sun god, was said to have descended from the skies to stand beside the virgin chosen to be his mother. "My soul is in him," declared the Deity, and thus one of the greatest of the Pharaohs was conceived.

These are myths, certainly, but they serve to emphasize the story of the fabulous birth of Melchizedek in The Secrets of Enoch (71). This was indeed one of the "secrets" unknown to the western world during the twelve centuries in which the book was "lost." It complements the lofty position given the high priest in both the Old Testament (the revered friend of Abraham) and the New (the prototype of Jesus Christ).

Canon Charles was inclined to consider the Melchizedek story an interpolation in The Secrets of Enoch, though reassured by the Slavic authority, Sokolov, that it was an "organic factor" in manuscript *A*. Firm in his own opinion, however, the Canon relegated Melchizedek to the appendix of the first English edition (1896), and dropped it altogether in the second (1912). He later incorporated Noah's birth from First Enoch.

Counterbalancing this scholarly determination (scholars can be just as opinionated as ignoramuses), Vaillant, in his 1952 translation of The Secrets of Enoch, restored the birth narrative of Melchizedek as the "organic factor" Sokolov maintained it was. (An interested reader of our present book might turn to chapter 71 of The Secrets of Enoch, which concludes this work, for comparison with the account of Noah's birth given in the next chapter.)

The late Dr. Rudolph Otto, one of the most penetrating German theologians of the twentieth century, in his profound study, *The Kingdom of God and the Son of Man* (1938), asks himself: "Where did the roots lie of the supernatural conception of Christ?" and answers that the historical connection had first been formed in circles in which Enoch's tradition was current. Appraising The Secrets of Enoch, Otto sees in the miraculous birth of Melchizedek an indication that "a type of Christ was soon to be recognized."

He considers the motivation for the phenomenon to be obvious: "The bearer of the renewed high priesthood [Melchizedek] is too holy a figure to issue from man's act. He must have his origin in the immediate miracle of God."

This presents a further problem: If Jesus was the author of The Secrets of Enoch, why did he substitute Melchizedek's birth for Noah's in his adaptation of the seer's work? An attempt will be made later in this book to provide an answer within the limits of this theory.

CHAPTER 9

The Two Enochs, Jesus, and Qumran

Incredible though the discovery of the Dead Sea
Scrolls was, causing international excitement, their contents proved even more astonishing. One of the finds was
a manuscript of the Book of Isaiah, practically intact, and older by a thousand years than any other that
had ever come to light. Other scrolls, only slightly dam-
aged by time, documented the daily life and the religious
doctrines of the ascetic sect that lived at Qumran for
almost two hundred years before the Roman Tenth Legion destroyed the settlement and the monastery in
A.D. 68.

Other scrolls and countless fragments of ancient biblical and pseudepigraphic writings were brought to light
in that desolate region to which the pious had once fled
from a wicked, godless world that faced imminent destruction. They were to spend the rest of their days in
prayer. According to the unearthed Manual of Discipline,
a most important and revealing sectarian document, they
were a strictly organized, monastic community. Member-

ship was for life, and property was owned communally (as was the custom among early Christians—except that with the Christians pooling was obligatory and voluntary).

After several years of search, eleven caves have yielded a tremendous store of manuscript remains. Cave 4 alone yielded fragments of no less than sixty manuscripts of books of the Bible. It is estimated that hundreds of manuscripts are represented; about two thirds of them are noncanonical, or pseudepigraphical.

The assembling of these countless fragments will prove a labor of Hercules. Thousands of the fragments are no bigger than a fingernail. Extreme delicacy, precision, learning and no end of patience will be required. Few men are equipped to put together this gigantic jigsaw puzzle, and fewer still are willing to undertake it. J. H. Allegro, an English scholar who gave himself up to the task, describes it in *The Dead Sea Scrolls*:

> "Hundreds of tiny fragments . . . must be laid out and minutely examined in the hope that they may connect with parent documents in reconstructing broken passages. . . . The fragments have to be cleaned of the white dust with which most are covered. Sometimes this is so finely ingrained that no amount of brushing will remove it. . . . Very often it is not so much the dust that obliterates the writing as the color of the leather itself, which has gone completely black from exposure to the humidity. . . . In these cases the process of infrared photography has been particularly valuable in our work. . . . The clean fragments are laid out between glass plates, several dozen or scores in each . . . over which he [the worker] will be spending the next year or two of his life crouching, trying to pick out pieces belonging to his documents, or seeking to identify new fragments. . . . He may find himself at the Aramaic text of a pseudepigraphical work never before seen in its original tongue, and all around him

will be biblical texts older by a thousand years
and more than Hebrew manuscripts of the Bible
previously known . . . but the way to revealing its
treasures is a hard one."

These dedicated scholars must not only piece together
bushels of papyrus and leather fragments, but also de-
cipher and translate eight different languages—and then
probably engage in hot debate over the interpretation of
an ancient word or phrase.

But that will be only the beginning of discovery and
debate. Was the Qumran sect Essene or not? Do the evident resemblances in idea and word between their sectarian documents and the New Testament indicate a
close relationship? These will be the prime issues. Arguments pro and con are already filling books—and there
are more to come.

My own stand has been made clear in earlier chapters. From obvious evidence, Jesus knew the Old Testament and the apocryphal literature as well as any Essene. The striking similarity of his thoughts and words to
those of the sect does not seem to have been fortuitous.
It is suspected that Jesus, as well as John the Baptist, had
an unrecorded but more or less intimate contact with the
Essenes. This supposition has the stronger basis with regard to John, because as a boy he went into the desert to
live (Luke 1:80). But where, exactly?

Many modern biblical scholars agree that the Essenes
followed a practice of "adopting" promising boys to in-
struct them in their doctrines and to take them into the
order. These young catechumens had to undergo severe
discipline—physical, mental and spiritual—until the age
of twenty. Then, after two years' further preparation,
they became candidates for the final oath of the humble,
flesh-mortifying brotherhood that expected hourly the
coming of the Kingdom of God. ("Repent, for the Kingdom of God is at hand!" both John and Jesus proclaimed.)

The Jewish historian Josephus (A.D. 37-95), describes

how he lived among the Essenes for three years, and observed their customs, habits and peculiar religious rites in worship and in ceremonial lustrations. Water was their symbol and agent of holy purification. Of their child-adoption practice, he wrote: "They reject pleasure as an evil and esteem continence and the conquest over our passions to be a virtue. They neglect wedlock, but choose out other persons' children, while they are pliable, and fit for learning; and esteem them to be of their children, and form them according to their own manners."

Because of their fairly close proximity to the Qumran monastery (the baptism of Jesus by John took place only a few miles away), both Jesus and John could have been most desirable additions to the Essene community. John was the son of a priest—which would have exerted a strong appeal to the pious sect. Jesus, his cousin, had a saintly aura about him and an irresistible magnetism that drew people to him. Possibly, too, rumors had reached Qumran that this unusual lad had held discussion with a learned group of elders in the Jerusalem Temple.

Most modern scholars scoff at any connection of consequence between the Essenes and Jesus and John and dismiss the Jordan baptism as merely circumstantial. It is their scholarly right to dismiss the theory as untenable, but if a still-hidden scroll relating something of the kind were to turn up some day, what would the pundits say or unsay? Meticulously built word-castles would tumble, and the very foundations of the Christian Church would tremble.

Aside from this controversial question of the relationship of Jesus to the Essenes, my conviction of the relation of Jesus to The Secrets of Enoch isn't lessened a jot by the respected observation of the late eminent Dr. W. F. Albright. Referring to the New Testament writers quoting Jesus, he said, "They drew from a common reservoir of terminology and ideas which were all well known to the Essenes and presumably familiar also to other Jewish sects of the period." Isn't there a touch of casuistry here?

Whether there is or not, the Dead Sea Scrolls and the Nag-Hammadi manuscripts discovered in an Egyptian tomb have alerted the intelligent public and the responsible press to the necessity for a fresh, unbiased appraisal of late pre-Christian Judaism and Christian origins, and, perhaps most important, a re-evaluation of the Christian literature of the first and second centuries. Christianity has become so socialized and psychoanalyzed that it might be a good idea to go back to basic principles.

Bible texts have been "modernized" into interpretative prose at the cost of poetic imagery, and careful addition of apocryphal matter, prayerfully chosen, would illuminate and enrich the whole. Legitimate, for instance, would be the selection of parts of the Enochan writings, inasmuch as Jesus and Paul, together with later Church Fathers, held several of these pseudpigraphic books to be on a par with inspired Scripture. Jesus and Paul were familiar with Enoch's Paradise and the seven heavens, and the great seer is mentioncd in both the Epistle of Jude and the Epistle to the Hebrews.

Fragments of ten different copies of First Enoch *in the original Aramaic* (not Ethiopic) have been identified in the Qumran manuscripts, which would indicate that he held a high position in the sect. Not a vestige of The Secrets of Enoch has yet materialized. It is my fervent hope that the search for more scrolls in the regional caves may bring to light a bit of The Secrets of Enoch— an authenticated sentence or two would suffice. A number of investigators agree that both First Enoch and The Secrets of Enoch were originally written by the Qumran Essenes, for the sect had a well-known penchant for pseudepigrapha (as evidenced in the Dead Sea Scrolls).

On the other hand, many of our leading scholars and theologians are reluctant to admit that Jesus ever came under the influence of the Essenes in any way. Some have been inclined to deny that Qumran was a community of Essenes because of certain deductions derived from factors attributable to one or other contemporary sects—Pharisees, Sadducees, Samaritans or Zealots, five sects that stem from Maccabean times.

Indeed, the Essenes became a closed subject for many biblical scholars at the end of the nineteenth century, when the highly cerebral Bishop Lightfoot of the Anglican Church killed the long-discussed theory of the Essene origin of Christianity. But the study of the Dead Sea Scrolls has brought the dead argument to life again, and a fresh battle is beginning. The opening gun was fired by Edmund Wilson, in his arousing account of the exhumed treasure, when he said it looked to him as though the Essenes were the cradle of Christianity. Perish the thought! cried the opposition, and wielded their fountain pens, or hammered typewriter keys.

The Enochan writings, especially The Secrets of Enoch, are on the side of Mr. Wilson. Though "lost" for centuries, these works reappeared in plenty of time to bear witness to whatever the Dead Sea Scrolls revealed of the period between Malachi and Matthew. History may never tell us why both the Enochan books were "lost." The one clue we do have is that the Ethiopic Enoch was in all probability taken to Abyssinia by the Ethiopian eunuch who was converted to Christianity by Philip (Acts 8). Authorities on the pseudepigrapha do not think the original texts suffered in translation to any important degree. Canon Charles gives his opinion of First Enoch: "It came from many writers and almost as many periods. It touches upon every subject that could have arisen in the ancient schools of the prophets, but naturally it deals with these subjects in an advanced stage of development. Nearly every religious idea appears in a variety of forms, and in the age to which the Enochan literature belongs, there is movement everywhere." The eminent scholar estimated the latest date of its composition at 64 B.C. In contrast to the multiple authorship of First Enoch, Canon Charles said that The Secrets of Enoch was, from all signs, the work of *one* writer, and conjectured he might have been a Hellenized Jew.

To begin with, First Enoch is about twice as long as

The Secrets of Enoch; it covers far more subject matter and is veritably omniscient. It is divided into five books. (The Jews of the day preferred sacred works in five divisions; the Torah, Proverbs and the Psalms are all thus divided.) The five books of Enoch are:

I: Describes his journey into other worlds under the informative guidance of an escort of angels, including his visit to Sheol, the place of departed spirits, good and bad; also describes many secrets of Nature and her laws.

II: Entitled The Second Vision of Wisdom, it contains the apocalyptic similitudes or parables. There are three: the first recounts the mysteries of the heavens; the second is devoted to the Messiah—his nature, purpose and role in the Last Judgment (intimating that he, Enoch, might be God's Anointed).

III: A long and labored "scientific" astronomical discourse on the heavenly bodies, with reckonings of the movements of sun and moon. (In the light of today's knowledge, this is, of course, infantile babbling.)

IV: An allegorical summary of world history, from Creation to the writer's own times.

V: Entitled The Apocalypse of Weeks (with the determination of a "week" left to the reader), it foretells (the narrator presumably goes back to Genesis) the Hebrew history up to the Exile. The Flood takes place in the second "week." The birth of Noah, however, is not given in its chronological order but at the end of the seventh "week." Here is the First Enoch account of Noah's nativity (replaced by Melchizedek's in The Secrets of Enoch):

> "And after some days my son Methuselah took a wife for his son Lamech, and she became pregnant by him, and gave birth to a son . . . and his father Lamech was afraid of him and fled, and came to his father Methuselah. And he said to him: I have begotten a strange son, unlike a man, and resembling the sons of the God of heaven; and his nature is different, and he is not like us and his eyes are as the

rays of the sun, and his countenance is glorious. And it seems to me that he is not sprung from me but from the angels and I fear that in his days a wonder may be wrought on the earth. And now, my father, I am here to petition thee and implore thee that thou mayest go to Enoch, our father, and learn from him the truth, for his dwelling-place is among the angels. And when Methuselah heard the words of his son [he] cried aloud, I came to him and said, Behold, here I am, my son, wherefore hast thou come to me? And he answered, Because of a great cause of anxiety have I come to thee. And now, my father, hear me. [Lamech tells of his fears.]

"And I, Enoch, answered, and said to him: The Lord will do a new thing on the earth, and this I have already seen in a vision. . . . Yea, there shall be a great destruction over the whole earth, and there shall be a deluge. . . . And this son who has been born unto you shall be left on the earth, and his three children shall be saved with him. And now make known to thy son Lamech that he who has been born to him is in truth his son, and call his name Noah. . . . He, the Lord, has shown me and instructed me, and I have read the tablets of heaven."

Naturally, in his description of the "end of days," First Enoch is in perfect accord with his eschatological fellow writers in depicting the horrors of eternal agony for sinners and the ineffable bliss for the righteous. That was the familiar grand finale of Hebrew prophecy, but Enoch, against all precedent, dared see himself as the potential Messiah! One can easily imagine the rage of the orthodox Jews. Not even the ranting, half-crazed wayside preachers predicting Judgment Day went that far. Enoch was wonderful, the populace thought, but hardly up to that extreme height of holiness. Maybe that was one of the reasons why he got "lost." Significant in that regard, too, were the objections of some Church Fathers to the inclusion of Jude in the canon of the New Testament because Enoch was mentioned in the fourteenth verse of that shortest of Epistles.

Nevertheless, in spite of ecclesiastical opposition, both Jewish and Christian, Enochan literature continued to be read and discussed by the common people. The very name Enoch exerted an irresistible appeal, even when it was a nom de plume. He "walked with God" and was transported to heaven without seeing death (Genesis 5:24) and was "seventh from Adam."

Revered and sanctified as the patriarchal name was, the leaders of the Synagogue and the early Christian Church would feel happier in the absence of the disturbing Enoch. How he was eventually "lost" would make an interesting story, but we cannot pause to evolve a theory. Instead, following the example of fine scholars whose knowledge and creative imagination defy accepted interpretation of a dim, enigmatic phase of the past, I propose to enter the arcna where "angels fear to tread." The miracle-filled atmosphere of our endeavor urges us on.

It has been shown that there is considerable difference in the respective lengths of the two Enochs, owing to the eliminations and condensations and the singular change in birth narratives. Particularly curious is the omission of the Book of Parables, acclaimed as the finest portion of First Enoch. Again and again, I tried to imagine why, gave up, then became fascinated with a recurrent picture.

Let us go back in imagination to the Qumran monastery of, say, the year A.D. 20. Under the supervision of a white-robed, austere, elderly teacher, a radiant, dark-eyed stripling is writing a thesis required for admission into the ascetic brotherhood, which solemn ceremony is set for the beginning of the new year. The boy has been a catechumen there since finishing his schooling at the synagogue. He's been a bright, extraordinarily intelligent student, but he's also been difficult to mold. The stern legalism of the Essene sect has troubled him. As a Galilean, the youth isn't a typical, strict Jew; some of the doctrines taught in the monastery haven't appealed to his innate sense of brotherly love and heavenly justice. As he comes into manhood, the Qumran belief that two Messiahs—one of Aaron's line, the other of Israel—will appear on the Great Day of Judgment creates growing doubt. His instructor has had to hold a tight rein on the keen, analytical boy.

Now he voices a troubled thought as he discusses his half-finished thesis with the white-robed superior: "We are taught to believe in two Messiahs as part of our oath when we are admitted, Nathan ben Shimon, and here Enoch intimates that he may be the Anointed One. I do not understand how that can be."

"My son, the ways of Yahweh are inscrutable," says the white-robed teacher sternly. "And His wisdom is not to be questioned."

"But we read in the Scriptures, honored sir, that there is but one Messiah," contends the young man from Nazareth. "I am confused, and beg your indulgence."

"I'm dutybound, my son, to bring you up before the Holy Council," says the instructor. "You still need more prayer and new penance."

According to the rules in the Manual of Discipline, the offender is punished. Apparently intransigent, the Nazarene omits the Enochan Parables from his thesis and, as an apologetic gesture, substitutes the birth of Melchizedek for that of Noah. The elect at Qumran, it will be remembered, called themselves the Sons of Zadok (Melchizedek).

Jesus of Nazareth may not have been admitted to the rigid order. Or, he could have resolved of himself not to submerge his spirit in a sect that cut itself off from the world in the selfish hope of exclusive salvation, and believed in loving friends but hating enemies.

Which action took place, we do not know. But all of us know that Jesus Christ gave himself to the world of mankind, even to death. There was nothing Essenic about that.

In connection with our imagined Qumran episode, it

is meet for us to add that the student-rebel may have been stirred by a premonitory feeling—indefinable, but strong—when he thought of the sacred conception of the Messiah, God's own emissary. How could anyone assume the tremendous role to himself! He loved Enoch and could accept his wondrous inspirations, but not this one. Indeed, the revered seer himself wasn't altogether clear or sure in his assumption.

Always, Jesus himself was reticent and evasive about claiming to be the Messiah. Whenever his disciples brought up the question, their Master chose to pacify their curiosity by referring to himself as the Son of Man, a title that had been applied to Ezekiel, and didn't necessarily mean the Son of God.

The way in which he parried the same urgent inquiry from John the Baptist is a striking example of his reservation on the subject. Jesus held no living man in higher estimation than John, who was lying in a dungeon at the time, doomed to be beheaded. John sent two of his faithful followers to ask the wonder-working prophet: "Art thou he that should come, or do we look for another?" (Luke 7:19). Jesus, in reply, told the messengers to watch him while he taught and healed and, after they had done so, he said, "Go your way and tell John what things ye have seen and heard; how that the blind see, the lame walk, the lepers are cleansed, the deaf hear, the dead are raised."

In other words, "Judge for yourself, John."

Jesus may have been waiting for some mysterious word or sign to declare himself "the Anointed." It was too fearful and marvelous a thought to entertain, let alone utter. Eventually, Simon Peter proved to be the agent of revelation in the famous scene at Caesarea Philippi, when Jesus asked his disciples: "Whom do men say that I the Son of Man am? And they said, Some say that thou art John the Baptist: some Elias; and others Jeremias or one of the prophets. He saith unto them, But whom say ye that I am? And Simon Peter answered and said, Thou art the Christ, the Son of the living God.

And Jesus answered and said unto him, Blessed art thou, Simon Bar-jona: for flesh and blood hath not revealed it unto thee, but my Father which is in heaven" (Matthew 16:13-16).

Equally humble and gentle, the author of The Secrets of Enoch, unlike Daniel and kindred writers who dealt with the "end of days," does not dwell on the everlasting punishment of sinners in fires of torment but emphasizes the rewards of the righteous, who "shall escape the Lord's Great Judgment and be called to Eternity, and at the same time Eternity will be joined to the just, and they will be immortal. And for them thereafter there will be no more weariness, neither suffering, nor sorrow, nor expectation of violence, neither any more misery of the night and dread of darkness. But they shall have a Great Light at all times, and an indestructible wall of Defense, and they shall have a Great Paradise, shelter for an everlasting habitation." (Second Enoch 66:8-10).

Christlike?

CHAPTER 10

Teachers of Righteousness

Newspaper stories and grapevine rumors spread concern when the discovery of the Dead Sea Scrolls was reported. Worry and incredulity grew as reliable reports verified the amazing find.

"What does it all mean?" people asked one another. "I can't believe that they go back two thousand years!"

"They don't," said the sophisticated and cynical. "It's just another hoax."

Anxiously, church members inquired of priests and pastors: "Is it going to change our belief in the divinity of Christ and in immortality?"

Said others, dismayed: "Was Jesus only a teacher of righteousness in a monastery in a desert of Judea?" (That had been suggested by a European biblical authority.)

In good time, reassurances came from scholars and historians who were studying and interpreting the Scroll texts. They confirmed that the Scrolls were genuine in their reported age and thus of priceless value. But none saw in them any threat to the Christian religion or to the validity of its founder. On the contrary, new and important light was shed on the Bible, and the identification of Jesus with the Teacher of Righteousness of the Qumran sect was proved entirely erroneous, for the latter died long before the former was born. And that was that.

Then who was this remarkable Teacher (he was nameless) who inspired his followers, led them into the desert, taught them the way of holy living and of God's intentions for mankind? Apparently, although unknown to history, he was a religious leader of some stature, the central figure of a dramatic conflict and possible tragedy.

Scholars are compelled to draw their different conclusions from the merest hints of his fate. Only once in the exhumed Qumran sectarian documents is he mentioned directly—that is in the Damascus (Zadokite) Document, in which he is described as "gathered in" (a phrase intimating death). Oddly, he isn't mentioned at all in the very important Manual of Discipline, which records the life and rules of the community. Naturally, the investigating experts expected that one so prominent and dominant would appear there, if anywhere.

This led some of them to subscribe to the idea that the Teacher of Righteousness wasn't any particular individual, but the title of an office occupied by the head of this religious order. This would mean that there had been a succession of these "Teachers" during the course of the approximately two hundred years of the sect's existence in the Judean Desert.

Yes, but who was *the* Teacher of Righteousness, he who had led a small group of Jewish dissidents, out of harmony with the Temple because of its desecration under the Hasmoneans, into the barren wilderness, where at first they had had to live in caves? Why was his identity veiled in such secrecy, and why was he alluded to as *the Priest, the Lawgiver,* or *the Star*? Dupont-Sommer, the eminent French scholar, explains: "His name is unknown. As a mark of respect, his adherents refrained from uttering it or writing it, just as the Jews then did with regard to the name of Yahweh . . . a name shrouded in mystery, a name which human lips are unworthy to pronounce."

Other, more matter-of-fact commentators conclude that the original Teacher wrote most of the documents of the Qumran community and felt no reason to name himself, that he was recording matters of daily life and religious doctrine and rites. Nameless he remains, though some scholars surmise that he might have been Onias, the last high priest of the Zadok line who was exiled and murdered in 175-174 B.C. Whether this leader and first Teacher survived this date is not known, or whether the "Wicked Priest" of the Hasmonean dynasty brought about his death and when. But the Scroll scholars generally agree that the unidentified hero assumed Essene leadership about 176 B.C. Baffling, too, is the identity of the "Wicked Priest," the villain of the piece: Who was *he*? And exactly why did he seek the life of the Teacher of Righteousness?

Putting on their deepest-thinking caps, the scholars set about solving the mystery. Eventually, they deduced that lethal attacks on sacerdotal personages above the law took place during three periods: in the first half of the second century B.C., during the rule of Antiochus Epiphanes; a century later, when Alexander Jannaeus was on the throne; and somewhat later, in the time of Aristobulus and Hyrcanus II, toward the middle of the first century B.C. Briefly, it was the Maccabean era of monstrous Hasmonean high-priest rulers, who were a bad lot, historically.

The scholars chose their "Wicked Priests," and advanced learned reasons for the selection. At bottom, it was speculation based on inferential evidence. However, it was undeniable fact that every one of their candidates was a supreme sadist, who treated the Jews inhumanly. Antiochus Epiphanes had made the practice of their revered religion a capital crime, and hanged circumcized babies around the necks of their crucified parents. His Hasmonean successors followed his fiendish example. Alexander Jannaeus, for instance, once ordered the crucifixion of some eight hundred alleged conspirators and had his victims' families slain before their dying eyes. Terrified Jews fled Jerusalem by the thousands—among them, most likely, the Teacher of Righteousness and his followers, who headed for the desert. There, they found shelter in caves, and began building quarters on the site of an old ruin which dated back to the eighth century B.C. To the cistern they found there they added others, starting their remarkable waterworks. More disaffected orthodox Jews joined them, and the isolated colony grew apace. Apparently, the "Wicked Priest" descended on the exiles, intent on killing the "Teacher," but the Qumran records do not state that he accomplished his evil deed. But if the assaulter was Alexander Jannaeus, we are told by Josephus that he died from a long drawn-out disease brought on by drunkenness and debauchery.

Meanwhile the Qumran community found peace and prosperity under the guidance of their holy leader, whose lofty ideal is expressed in the Manual of Discipline, then known as the Rule of the Community:

> "To enlighten the heart of Man and to make straight before him all the ways of true righteousness, to make his heart fearful of the judgments of God; a humble spirit, an even temper, a freely compassionate nature, and eternal goodness, and understanding and insight, and mighty wisdom which believes in all God's works, and a confident trust in His many mercies, and a spirit of knowledge in every ordered work . . . and a radiant purity which loathes every impure idol; a notable bearing and a discretion regarding all the hidden things of Truth and secrets of Knowledge."

This noble plan, it is estimated, was set down in the second century B.C., in the era when the Teacher of

Righteousness was "raised up" by God to save his leader-less schismatics from destruction. Possibly, he was influenced in his high idealism by the then widely-read First Enoch. At least, his words echo the seer who became one of the Essene "saints."

The daily program of work, prayer, purification and communal unity of the Qumranians differed a great deal from the basic pattern of current rabbinical teaching derived from Mosaic Law. There was, however, one striking ritual of the cenobites that resembled the sacred meal (Eucharist) of bread and wine, later instituted by the early Christian Church. They called it a "Messianic Banquet," a rehearsal of the future feast to be shared when the two Messiahs they looked for arrived and sat down with them in a holy celebration of the Great Day appointed by Yahweh. But it would be stretching a point to find resemblance between this and the Christian Eucharist, for the mystery religions of the time always included ceremonial banquets in their services. Wine was considered the drink of the gods and drunk in reverential libation.

Aside from this universal practice, the scholars studying the Dead Sea Scrolls find, as they no doubt expected, that there is constant confirmation of the fact that early Christians naturally adopted and incorporated earlier religious ideas and forms, particularly those of the Jewish Essenes. More important, they gave to these ideas and forms a new dynamism. For the Qumran leader, "to whom God made known all the mysteries of the words of the prophets" (to quote the Manual again), was an inspired man; he was not to be compared with Jesus, whose destiny, as he said, was "to overcome the world." The Teacher of Righteousness and his flock vanished from earth; his influence, if any, continues through the New Testament in Jesus' words.

But the Qumran leader was a notable poet and psalmist, as the Thanksgiving Hymns testify. (These were found on a scroll in Cave 1, as was the Manual of Discipline, and were given this title by the late Professor E. L. Sukenik, who was the first to translate the devotional poems into English.) Besides the author's perpetual refrain of thanks to God, tiny glimpses of autobiography are supposedly ascribed to him. The following are brief excerpts:

"For he has driven me from my country like a bird
    from its nest.
All my friends and acquaintances were thrust afar
    from me.
    And they thought I was like a lost vessel.
And they, the interpreters of lies and prophets of
    guile,
    They formed against me plots of Belial [Satan],
Wanting me to barter Thy law which Thou hast en-
    graved on my heart
For the flatteries which they address to Thy peo-
    ple."

Also this "personal" touch:

"And I became . . . an object of quarrel and strife
    among my friends,
Jealousy and anger to those who entered my cove-
    nant,
And all those who assembled around me grumbled
    and complained. . . .
Those who eat my bread lifted up their head against
    me,
And all those who joined my party have cast
    aspersions upon me
And the men of my community turned rebellious
    and grumbling round about."

"And I have been a snare for sinners,
But healing for all those that are converted from
    sin,
Prudence for the simple

And the firm inclination of all those whose heart
    is troubled.
And Thou hast made of me an object of shame and
    mockery for traitors."

Most of the hymns begin with "I give Thee thanks, O
Adonai." Their lyricism in general draws on the canonical Psalms, and occasionally on Jeremiah and Job. Nevertheless, a strong, vibrant personality comes through the
lines.

While crediting the Teacher of Righteousness with
authorship of the Essene sectarian documents, scholars
have decided that he could not have written the War of
the Sons of Light Against the Sons of Darkness because
they date it as a number of years after his death. This
scroll, one of the finds of 1947, was titled by Dr. Sukenik
and translated by his son, Yagael Yadin, an Israeli army
colonel.

Unlike any other Qumran scroll, this presents a carefully worked-out military campaign for that greatest of
all battles of the forces of Good and Evil anticipated for
the "end of days," a battle which might last forty years
(a favorite Old Testament figure). The planner, though
copying Roman military strategy, included songs and
prayers to be offered up at certain junctures. Such a terrific encounter was a common eschatological conception
of the pseudepigraphic scribes, and was to be immortalized in the Book of Revelation.

According to the Essene program, their worshiped
Teacher of Righteousness was to return to earth before
this Armageddon as the interpreter of the Law. Certainly, the Qumran sect was to be well provided for in
the Grand Finale, having two Messiahs and their angelic
Teacher. It does not appear that the Teacher, in his lifetime, ever laid claim to any major apocalyptic role, which
he could have done as one in the confidence of God,
even as Enoch assumed Messiahship.

Nor was Enoch alone in that period of "false prophets," against whom Christ often warned his hearers.

These were typical of Galilee, where Jesus began his ministry. They were commonly alluded to as *ober gelila'ah* (Galilean itinerants). They may be likened to those biblical exhorters who once traveled from village to village, preaching fire and brimstone if sinners did not repent. Now, their well-meaning messages are painted on roadside rocks, or urged on radio broadcasts for those who love just retribution.

It was in the land of the *ober gelila'ah* that Jesus first proclaimed the Kingdom of God, after his baptism in the Jordan and forty days' temptation by the Devil in the Judean Desert. Galilee was then a liberal, open-hearted country through which a variety of pilgrims journeyed to Syria and beyond. The land was lively; the natives were only mildly orthodox, inclined to be unprejudiced religiously. The mysticism of the East was more or less familiar to them, and came by way of Babylonian Judaism, born during the Exile. So they were fully conditioned to apocalyptic preaching.

The message brought by Jesus to Galilee had elements of Persian doctrine which, if analyzed, could be traced back to ancient Aryan theology. For that matter, Ezekiel had led the way centuries before. The teaching of Jesus held a more universal outlook than that of the average preacher. Therefore, his discourses struck a new note in liberal-minded Galilee. We may imagine that Enoch was ever present in his thought, coloring it now and then, perhaps. No doubt his interested audiences often wondered where this eloquent Nazarene—not a learned rabbi but a simple carpenter—got some of his arresting ideas about life here and hereafter. And they whispered fearfully to one another of the wonders he performed. Crowds followed him wherever he went. No other *ober gelila'ah* ever spoke like this. His parables were beyond any that they had ever heard from even the finest rabbis.

Indeed, Jesus knew the Law and the Prophets by heart, together with the revelations of Enoch and his fellow scribes, whose aim was to comfort and sustain downtrodden Israel. Enoch passed on to Jesus the influence of the great Persian prophet Zoroaster (circa 660-583 B.C.) in much of his vision of the coming of the Kingdom of God. Similarly, the Essenes assimilated in their doctrines this eastern representation of the "end of days." There was the cosmic conflict between Good or Light (Ahura Mazdah) and Evil or Darkness (Angra Mainyu), resurrection from the dead, final Judgment, and a "wondrous new creation" of the world. Of course, Zoroastrianism was but a part of Jesus' teaching.

Supreme teachers of righteousness have been few in history, and for his effect on Christ and—through Christ's ministry—on us, we feel inclined to number Enoch among them. From chapter 12 on of First Enoch, there are many ethical exhortations and sermons, and in The Secrets of Enoch there are maxims and parables that seem the product of the same mind incorporated in the New Testament.

That Enochan literature was the medium of Zoroastrianism into later Judaism is evident in chapter 24 of The Secrets of Enoch. Surely, it is more like Ahura Mazdah than Yahweh to express the desire to confide in the seer the secret of his immortal nature for the first time in Eternity, when not even the angels knew its "boundlessness and its incomprehensibility."

Let us go back to the decisive moment we imagined, when Jesus refused to accept his admired Enoch as the Messiah. He was a mere youth then, but what were his reflections afterward? Had his demonstrated power over the minds and bodies of people stirred any Messianic consciousness within himself? In the Gospels he avoids the issue as long as he can. Ambiguously, he calls himself the Son of Man, but gives no definite impression until the end that he would be the *Christus designatus,* chosen by God Himself.

Throughout the few years of his ministry, Jesus frequently intimated that the Kingdom of God had already begun but was to be fully established in eschatological terror and grandeur. If, as has been suggested by some scholars, the "Little Apocalypse" of Mark 13 is an interpolation, then Christ said a minimum on the awesomeness of the Last Judgment, leaving that to the professional apocalyptists.

Aside from phenomena of sacrificial atonement for the sins of the world, his resurrection and ascension, the miracles of his ministry have been most doubted through the centuries. Seldom, if ever, is Jesus' charismatic power taken into account, because its action is put on par with superstitious magic, or hypnotism, or autosuggestion, at best. But this is generally uninformed judgment. Science knows better.

What exactly is this charismatic power ascribed to Jesus Christ in the highest potentiality?

Ordinarily, it is associated with a holy man or saint who is apparently able to perform feats unaccountable by the laws of Nature. Psychology and psychiatry have tried, and are still trying, to define this quality in the human spirit, but modern skeptics doubt it exists—just as they dismiss belief in soul. Hysteria, delusion or fraud, say the materialistic savants.

Very good, but in the case of the extraordinary man, Christ, it would be only reasonable to pause and ask: Was this charismatic power merely imagined by his witnesses, or was it intrinsic to his transcendental character? At least, his gift was on a special plane. It is not to be compared with the "miraculous" operations of many rabbis and run-of-the-mill prophets recorded in ecclesiastical memorabilia and history; it emanated from his magnetic personality. Seemingly troubled himself at times by its exercise, Jesus habitually exacted a promise from those who benefited from his healing touch to say nothing about it. And it will be remembered how he rebuked the Pharisees who asked for a miraculous demonstration, stigmatizing them as of "an evil and adulterous generation."

More difficult still is to accept or explain how Jesus could impart charismatic power to his disciples for their missionary work. This power was also given to the Apostle Paul, although he never met the Master in the flesh. But we do know that *charism*, a Greek word, means *a favor specially vouchsafed by God*, and does not involve omnipotence or omniscience. Simply, it is a heightening of talents and capacities, such as are exhibited in inexplicable genius. Mathematics and music have given us famous examples. Prophecy, healing, exorcism and inspired preaching are psychologically considered to be the chief manifestations of this mysterious quality.

Whatever else he was, Jesus was the greatest charismatic ever known, whose unseen power—and this is miraculous in itself—is still undiminished. His last words before his ascension (Mark 16:17-18) were charismatic:

> "And these signs shall follow them that believe; in my name shall they cast out devils; they shall speak with new tongues; they shall take up serpents; and if they drink any deadly thing, it shall not hurt them; they shall lay hands on the sick, and they shall recover."

CHAPTER 11

"How Long, O Lord, How Long?"

Although their origins may be traced to the canonical prophets, psalmists and poets of the Old Testament, the apocalyptists differed considerably in their approach and presentation. They were fearless of sacred precedent, dared to "improve" on the Word, and borrowed the names of the most famous biblical characters as pseudonyms. If readers didn't always believe them, they enjoyed their fantastic variations with oriental appreciation. Doubtless, too, they were thrilled to read spicy morsels of what might be called gossip about the awesome patriarchs, such as were found in one of the commentaries among the Dead Sea Scrolls, known as Genesis Apocryphon.

One of the seven earliest-found manuscripts in Qumran's Cave 1, it told embellished stories of Abraham and Sarah in Egypt, where the Pharaoh fell in love with Abraham's beautiful wife, and most of the account of Noah's birth. Interestingly, the characters tell their stories in the first person—a modern touch on the part of the redactor of Genesis.

Born of prophecy, however, apocalypticism was mainly concerned with the world-reckoning Day of Yahweh, which the Jews awaited in longing and prayer, hope and fear through centuries of submission and suffering. All they saw was their cruel, sinning masters flourishing like the proverbial green bay tree, while the Chosen People remained chattel. When was the God of Abraham, Jacob and Isaac going to save them and make them a nation again? "How long, O Lord, how long?" was the cry sent up by generations of hearts and lips. History has never seen greater patience and faith in a people. It took more than two thousand years before Israel was restored to nationhood—strangely enough, at the same time that the Dead Sea Scrolls rose from their graves to bear witness, as it were, to final justice.

The great Judgment Day of Yahweh, so long in coming, had been envisioned as early as the eighth century B.C. by Amos and Isaiah, then continued by Zephaniah, Ezekiel, Joel to the climax of Daniel. Its basic pattern was the same—the nations of earth gathered together for everlasting punishment and reward according to their sins and virtues, Creation returned to Chaos. Zoroaster foresaw a similar fate for humanity, with a holocaust of rivers of fire. The prophet Jeremiah, though not classed as an apocalyptist, gives this vision of the aftermath of the Day of Yahweh (4:23-26):

> "I beheld the earth, and lo, it was without form, and void; and the heavens, and they held no light. I beheld the mountains, and lo, they trembled, and all the hills moved lightly. I beheld, and lo, there was no man, and all the birds of the heavens were fled. I beheld, and lo, the fruitful place was a wilderness, and all the cities thereof were broken down at the presence of the Lord, and by his fierce anger."

Jeremiah's lamentation is quietly mournful when compared to the fiery symbolism of Daniel and Revelation, which first came into Hebraic prophetic expression with Ezekiel, the prophet of the Exile, who adopted the religious imagery of Babylon. Ezekiel's innovation afforded apocalypticism a new and most effective "secret language," bringing to a peak the dynamism and significance of this depiction of the "end of days." Also, it aided enormously in the telling of the history of the wronged and persecuted Jews without disclosing the identity of the writer to the pagan overlords. Thus, white bullocks could represent patriarchs; wild animals, the despised Gentiles; the Egyptians were wolves; the Assyrians and Babylonians became lions and tigers; the Greek tyrants were fierce eagles, vultures and kites; the Jews themselves, blind sheep.

"In a Symbol," says Carlyle, "there is concealment and yet revelation: hence therefore, by Silence and by Speech acting together, comes a double significance."

Enoch certainly incorporated that profound mystical element in his prolific writings, which began in the last half of the third century B.C. At that time he, and others, began to speculate on a revolutionary idea: the individual resurrection of the body, but without definite relation to personal immortality.

Ideas of an afterlife were somewhat confused. Before the Exile there had been only nebulous outlines, though prophets and psalmists had spoken of eternal felicity with Yahweh. Isaiah had said, "Thy dead men shall live"; Ezekiel had described dried human bones clothing themselves with flesh; and the later Daniel said, "Many of them that sleep in the dust of the earth shall awake" (12:2).

Like their forefathers, the Jews of the intertestamental period continued to believe in Sheol (Enoch had described a visit there), where the dead continud to exist —although without life unless released by Yahweh. Abraham, Jacob, Isaac and other patriarchs were dead, nevertheless they "lived unto Him!" There was no record that they rose from their graves to be with their Maker.

What were the implications in the word *resurrection*? The Jews, like their forefathers, expected that they would be summoned and judged as a whole people, with everlasting life for individuals dimly discerned. It was hard to conceive of perpetuity except for the chosen spokesmen of the Most High.

Enoch further complicated the question when he referred to the raising of the dead in his description of the Last Judgment: "In those days the earth will give back whoever was assembled in her."

Well might the orthodox ask: Did "whoever" mean Gentiles, too? Was their hateful dust to be reanimated any more than that of beasts? No, utter obliteration should be their portion! Resurrected, they might war against Yahweh. Rabbinical search of the Scriptures failed to produce support for this monstrous idea.

But the indignant orthodox were to be affronted again by Enoch when he said there was to be not only physical resurrection but immortality as well, for all mankind, righteous and wicked. We can imagine the synagogue congregations up in arms at this terrible heresy. Why, the word of God itself had cursed the idol-worshiping heathen! How could Enoch, His confidant, make such a diabolic statement? Satan had beguiled the wonderful seer of Israel! The rabbis, who often deplored the arrogated omniscience of the pseudepigraphic writers and denounced their revelations, had found another grievance against them.

"Modern" theological thinkers would go along with Enoch and defend his transcendent wisdom, for as Ecclesiasticus declared, "Upon the earth, there is no man created like him." The anonymous scribes behind the mask of Enoch had shown an all-knowingness found in no other of their ilk. Ecclesiasticus was right.

According to tradition, before the eternal age arrived there were to be the "days of the Messiah," which were generally considered as forerunners of Finality—happy days for the Elect. But the fate of those who weren't in that category was left, more or less, to the imagination or to rabbinical interpretation. The Scriptures confined themselves to the Day of Yahweh. But, as usual, Enoch had his own farsighted version (that he might be right was not solacing to the weary masses): there were to be *two* Judgment Days for the world!

"How long, O Lord, how long?" would be the familiar cry to this.

Enoch referred sapiently to hallowed Genesis, in which the Creator made the world out of the void in six days, and rested the seventh. Under this simple statement was a hidden forecast of future history. If one day with God was equal to a thousand mortal years (Psalm 90:4), then the world was to endure for six thousand years. His "rest," therefore, was equivalent to one thousand years—the millennium—which would be a prelude of leisure and joy for mankind, after which Yahweh would rule forever and ever, amen. Enoch describes the cosmic event in these words for foes and friends:

> "The first heaven shall depart and pass away and a new heaven shall appear, and all the powers of the heavens shall give a seven-fold light; and after that there shall be many weeks without number for ever and ever, and all shall be goodness and righteousness, and sin shall be no more for ever."

The Jews were not a mathematical people, and Jewish reckoning of time was notoriously unreliable: a "day" might mean a thousand years, and the figure *40* was used for uncertain units. Enoch has an Apocalypse of Weeks in his fifth book, taking no account of sidereal time. His first "week" begins with the first chapter of Genesis; the second ends with the Flood; the third opens with the call of Abraham; the fourth relates to the giving of the Law to Moses and the formation of the nations; the fifth ends with the dedication of Solomon's Temple; the sixth ends with the capture of Jerusalem by Nebuchadnezzar; the seventh is concerned with the rebellion of the Jews against oppression and the coming of the Messiah; the eighth sees the judgment of the heathen by "the saints in glory"; the ninth ushers in the Reign of Righteousness revealed to all the world; and the tenth ushers in the Final Judgment and the hour of Eternity.

Presumably, Enoch's ninth week began the fabulous millennium, after the judgment by "the saints in glory," and that was the sticking point for the orthodox, high or humble. Besides the two judgments he proclaimed, Enoch had bewildered and awed them by mysteriously intimating that he was the potential Messiah! He said that God Himself had told him that in a vision, when a celestial figure, which had been before the foundation of the world, appeared. Addressing the Lord of Spirits (his name for Yahweh), Enoch inquires who he is and whence he came, and is told the celestial figure is *himself*, the Son of Man (the ambivalent term that did not necessarily mean the Son of God in its holiest of holy definitions).

Here, once more, attention must be called to the deep influence of Zoroastrianism on Enoch and his writings, and later, on Jesus. When he saw himself as the Son of Man, or the Messiah, Enoch was drawing upon the Iranian conception of the *fravashis*, the spiritual form of men created by Ahura Mazdah aeons before their flesh-and-blood counterparts. Scholars see the same Iranian source for the "Son of Man" in the Book of Daniel, possibly coeval with the "Parables" portion of First Enoch. (A much later date is given it by some commentators.)

The Old Testament prophets, in depicting the Day of Yahweh, never introduced an intermediary between God and man; the Messianic Kingdom was regarded as the fulfillment of the unwavering faith of the Chosen People in the national sublimation of Israel. The Anointed (Messiah) of the Lord God was prophesied, but there was no mention of a Son of Man. Daniel, who does mention a Son of Man, wasn't considered a prophet in the strict sense of Jewish classification.

Whether or not he upset the orthodox public with his radical ideas, Enoch's very name carried weight and cast a kind of spell that endures to the present day. His continuing influence is evident in the Seventh Day Adventists, who look for the Second Coming of Christ on a modern date. (They were commonly called Millennarians.)

Dante may be cited as following the pattern of Enoch's progressive journey from the Inferno to Paradise; and probably Milton, in *Paradise Lost*, owed Enoch something in his description of Lucifer, who was cast out of heaven for rebelling against the Almighty.

His fellow writers thought so highly of Enoch that they quoted him as an authority. Certainly, the Essenes were his devotees, as the Dead Sea Scrolls recently testified (fragments of ten copies of First Enoch were identified). Oddly, no trace of the "Parables" section (the same portion omitted by the author of The Secrets of Enoch) has yet come to light in the Scroll treasure. Such a discovery—especially if the section were in the original Aramaic, as are the fragments of its predecessor —would disprove Canon Charles' theory that it was written in Greek by a Hellenized Jew. It would also favor the theory of Jesus' authorship, though there is no doubt that Jesus could write in Greek, as he read the Septuagint in the synagogue. However, Canon Charles' enormous knowledge cannot be discounted and his description of Enoch as "the chief figure next to Daniel in Jewish apocalyptic prior to A.D. 49," who lost that position because the "Christians made too much of him," corroborates my theory of the orthodox Jewish reaction to some of Enoch's more sensational pronouncements.

But Enoch was in perfect accord with the New Testament and with the Essene documents, using the symbol of Light for Good (God) and Darkness for Evil (Devil), which he derived from the Iranian *Avesta* (Zoroaster's Bible). The Persian prophet says, "The two primal spirits [Mazdah and Ahriman] who revealed themselves in vision as twins are the Better [Light] and the Bad [Darkness] in thought, word and action. And between these two the wise know to choose aright, the foolish not so."

It is not out of keeping to suspect that the writings of Enoch in this connection may have influenced the Essenes. The Manual of Discipline, the Damascus Document, and the War of the Sons of Light Against the Sons of Darkness employ this symbolism repeatedly. Also, it appears in the three Synoptic Gospels, and notably in that of John (8:12, 14:17, 15:26, 16:13) and in John's first Epistle (4:6). Apostle Paul was fond of similar thought-form contrast (Romans 2:19 and 13:12; Ephesians 5:8 and 6:12; First Thessalonians 5:5).

In tune with the Infinite, as always, The Secrets of Enoch transports us to the highest heaven, quoting God's relation of the creation of man: "I showed him the two roads, the Road of Light and the Road of Darkness, and I said to him: This one is good and that one is evil, that I might learn if he has love for Me, or hate."

To the ancient Jewish cry, "How long, O Lord, how long?" has come a twofold answer: the State of Israel, after two thousand years, is a reality; and the Dead Sea Scrolls have risen out of the earth to bear witness.

Great is Yahweh.

CHAPTER 12

Learned and Lay Probings

Scholarly eyebrows and voices will be lifted at the very idea that Jesus Christ might have written anything, least of all a pseudepigraphical work. True, he is no longer held to be a mere carpenter, without much education; but, like Socrates, he was content to express his marvelous mind in speech. It was enough that he wrote on the hearts of men. Since the days of the Evangelists, thousands of books have been written about him, and virtually none consider him as an author of aught save the Kingdom of God and man's immortality. The reaction of the learned fellowship when *Did Jesus Write This Book?* comes to their critical attention can be predicted:

Q.: Whatever gave you the idea?

A.: Oh, it just came, I guess.

Q.: No authority?

A.: Only long intensive study, and the kind of intuition you scholars use with your knowledge.

Q.: I see, but both intuition, as you call it, and knowledge can arrive at wrong conclusions—even on the same subject.

A.: Yes, I've noted that in my research, and it is one of the great mysteries of the human mind how identical factors undergo such change in individual reaching of conclusion.

Q.: Perhaps you'll tell us why you chose The Secrets of Enoch out of the pseudepigrapha rather than, say, the Book of Jubilees or the Testaments of the Twelve Patriarchs?

A.: But don't you remember it's in this book we're discussing?

Q.: To be sure I do, but I thought you might have something else to add.

A.: Isn't it enough that Second Enoch was written in Jesus' own lifetime—that is, between A.D. 1 and 50, according to best authority?

Q.: Well, if that's so, why do you suppose that none of the Evangelists allude to such authorship on the part of their Master?

A.: I can only guess at the possible reason. The writers of pseudepigrapha wished to be unknown, for there was a price on their heads for publishing literature of this type, and we don't suppose for a moment the Evangelists would betray Jesus. Besides, these anonymous writings were beginning to lose favor with the public, according to Canon Charles, the expert on pseudepigrapha.

Q.: Very good, sir. But as a last point, I must ask you why it is that no modern scholar has discovered before now that Jesus may have been the author of The Secrets of Enoch?

A.: Possibly a matter of time. You know, The Secrets of Enoch was lost to the western world for some twelve hundred years, until brought to its attention in 1892 in the Slavonic tongue. The belief that it was merely a condensation of First Enoch could have dampened scholarly curiosity, or deferred its action.

But not mine. Having become a serious and enthusiastic student of apocalyptic Jewish literature, which grew to astonishing proportions during the few centuries between Malachi and Matthew, I set to work comparing the two Enochs and was struck by the omissions and emendations in the Slavonic version of the seer. It was fascinating to think that, despite its translation into Slavonic (and heaven only knows what other languages it had passed through since its disappearance), The Secrets of Enoch maintained this aura of the Gospels.

Then one day it struck me with fresh force that while First Enoch was the composite work of a number of writers, the eminent Canon Charles had said The Secrets of Enoch was the script of *one* author between the years A.D. 1 and 50. The Dead Sea Scrolls were then under scholarly scrutiny, and there was much discussion about Jesus' relationship with the Essenes. I remembered an arresting passage pertinent to that present discussion in J. E. H. Thomson's *Books Which Influenced Our Lord and His Apostles,* and reread it:

"There are several different kinds of Essenes. While there was a nucleus that kept the Essene vows with the greatest strictness, there was around this a large mass of sympathizers who were connected more or less loosely with the Essene society, and from these the central brotherhood was recruited. They came themselves, and took on the vows, or they devoted their children to the Essenes to be brought up by them. If, then, Joseph and our Lord's mother belonged to this outer circle of Essenes, Jesus' acquaintanceship with the Essene books becomes easily understood. . . . It would only be perhaps as a special act of favor that the sacristan would admit this strange youth to see these sacred books and peruse their contents. In the eventide, when perhaps there were no guests in the dwelling of the Essenes in Nazareth, the youth, with his lustrous eyes full of thought, would stop before the

narrow green side door that breaks the white sur-
face of the wall of the flat-roofed house near the
gate where the Essenes had their dwelling. It is
opened to him by the guardian, an old man, most
likely with long beard, clad in pure white garments,
who leads him away to the inner room, where, in a
scrinium or two, the scanty but precious library of
the house is kept. The swinging lamp is lit, and there
he sits and reads far into the night the strange visions
recorded in the Books of Enoch, or of Baruch."

Imaginative, yes, but it could have been true. I followed this provocative line of thought: Why couldn't that
studious youth have felt the urge to be a writer? It was
characteristic of Jews to record their history by memory
before the invention of calligraphy, and it was second
nature for a student to want to write. Why not Jesus
in those eighteen "silent" years? Even if he lived in
Nazareth during all that time—which in view of his mental and spiritual capacities is doubtful—he would have
been in contact with a somewhat cosmopolitan world.
There was a busy caravan route nearby between Syria
and Egypt, and from the travelers' encampments it
would be possible to gather a wide and varied picture
of other ways of life and ideas. Being a Galilean, Jesus
was not prejudiced against other peoples in favor of
Judaism. In fact, he loved the beauties of the world and
mankind.

This whirl of ideas, plus the news of increasing apposi-
tion of Jesus and the Essene sect at Qumran, stirred me
to real excitement: The Essenes were acknowledged to
be the encouragers par excellence of pseudepigrapha,
and some of these writings were produced in their head-
quarters. As the work on the Dead Sea Scrolls pro-
gressed, my hope that First Enoch and The Secrets of
Enoch would be found among them in the original
Aramaic or Hebrew mounted high. Such a discovery
would be of primary importance and would supersede
the Ethiopic and Slavonic translations. I was thrilled as

the news drifted in from Qumran. When the official word was given that it would probably take fifty years to complete the enormous task of piecing the fragments into a whole, I felt let down. But when it was reported that fragments of First Enoch had come to light in the original Aramaic, my hopes soared again—perhaps The Secrets of Enoch would be found, too. The matching of the fragments wasn't half completed, and the exploration of caves was continuing. There was plenty of time for the wish to come true.

Meanwhile, the two Enochs occupied my mind. As I pored over them, word for word, with the Gospels for reference (I had studied Greek, Hebrew and Aramaic, among other languages), I faced many problems of translation and transliteration. But the most perplexing question was: Why did the redactor of First Enoch scrap the Parables, leave out most of the Apocalypse of Weeks and substitute the birth of Melchizedek for that of Noah? This mental wrestling went on long before the sensational discovery of the Dead Sea Scrolls. The Qumran find became newspaper headlines, giving rise to rumors that Jesus and the Essene Teacher of Righteousness were one and the same! Of course, I knew that to be a foolish canard.

But couldn't Jesus, as well as John the Baptist, have been a student at the Qumran monastery? The Essenes followed the custom of adopting boys, and both boys lived not far from the settlement. Also, John had baptized Jesus in the Jordan, within a few miles of Qumran.

Flavius Josephus, the Jewish historian of the first century A.D., gave a detailed account of the Essenes' way of life, of which the following excerpt affords us a vivid glimpse:

> "Their piety towards the Deity takes a particular form: Before sunrise they speak no profane word but recite certain ancestral prayers to the sun as though entreating it to rise.
>
> "After these prayers the superiors dismiss them

so that each man may attend to the craft with which he is familiar. Then, after working without interruption until the fifth hour [about 11 A.M.], they reassemble in the same place and, girded with linen loincloths, bathe themselves thus in cold water. After this purification they assemble in a special building to which no one is admitted who is not of the same faith; they themselves only enter the refectory if they are pure, as though into a holy precinct.

"When they are quietly seated, the baker serves out the loaves of bread in due order, and the cook serves only one bowlful of one dish to each man.

"Before the meal the priest says a prayer and no one is permitted to taste the food before the prayer; and after they have eaten the meal he recites another prayer. At the beginning and end they bless God as the Giver of life.

"Afterwards they lay aside the garments which they have worn for the meal, since they are sacred garments, and apply themselves again to work until the evening.

"Then they return and take their dinner in the same manner, and if guests are passing through they sit at the table. No shouting or disturbance ever defiles the house; they allow each other to speak in turn.

"To those outside, the silence of the men inside seems a great mystery; but the cause of it is their invariable sobriety and the fact that their food and drink are so measured out that they are satisfied and no more!

"I think it is because of the simplicity of their way of life and their regularity that they live long, so that most of them reach the age of more than a hundred years."

Against this, I decided to check the doctrines and general activities set forth in their Manual of Discipline, which was one of the earliest of the Dead Sea Scrolls to be found. Fortunately, it was almost wholly intact, and was soon translated. From what I gathered, the Qumran monastery would have been more sympathetic schooling for John the Baptist than for Jesus. But if they had been catechumens there, why did they leave before full initiation into the brotherhood? For some unknown reason or impulse, John left to preach the Essenes' own doctrine of the "end of days," for which they watched hourly.

But why did young Jesus leave the pious fold? I cudgeled my brain for a logical, acceptable answer, and painstakingly examined all of the Essene sectarian documents published in English. I concluded that, in light of what is known of Jesus' character, he wouldn't have liked the religious exclusiveness practiced by the Essenes, who withdrew from the world to guarantee their *personal* salvation. Nor would he have accepted their requirement to love the righteous and condemn evildoers. Most of all, I thought, he would have repudiated their doctrine of *two* Messiahs, one of Aaron's priestly line, the other of Israel's idolized David. That was not scriptural, and Jesus knew every word of the Law and the Prophets from childhood, which is deducible from his arguments with the Jerusalem elders in the Temple as a boy of twelve (Luke 2:46-47).

Having always prided myself on my common sense and critical perception, I asked myself whether, in this pursuit of a beloved theory, I were not losing my sane balance in self-delusion.

Could be, but every time I read his nine beatitudes (Second Enoch 42) it seemed as if I could close my tired eyes and hear the far-off voice of Jesus delivering the Sermon on the Mount.

Often, people smiled indulgently at my enthusiastic expositions, but whether or not I was a victim of what is known as a "fixed idea," the clamor of public misunderstanding over the experts' interpretation of the religious significance of the Dead Sea Scrolls sent me promptly to the lecture platform to explain and clarify the welter of misled conclusions and contradictions in press and social gatherings.

I was pleased to discover that my audiences were intelligently interested and critical. They wanted to *know* the wheat from the chaff. It became advisable to distribute slips among the eager listeners for their written questions after my lecture. Nor was it unusual for sixty or seventy queries to be sent up to the platform speaker. Occasionally, a spoofer or smart-aleck would try to be cynical or funny, but the majority of the audience was earnest and serious. The following small collection of questions indicates that attitude:

"How much will the Bible have to be changed because of the new light shed on its text by the Scrolls? You tell us that already the Revised Version has incorporated corrections from the oldest copy of Isaiah that was found."

"Is it possible that the contents of the Dead Sea Scrolls may alter our centuries-old belief in the Scriptures?"

"I'm interested very much in the similarity of the religious rites practiced by the Essenes and early Christians. Will you tell us more about them?"

"The mutual symbolism recorded as between the Essenes and St. John, the Evangelist, is intriguing. Can you recommend a book on the subject?"

"Would you say that the Apocrypha should be officially restored to every Protestant Bible, and integrated in the text of the Book itself as in the Catholic version?"

"Evidently, you don't believe, Doctor, that Jesus was the reincarnation of the Essene Teacher of Righteousness. Why couldn't it be, as well as other miracles of the time?"

"Is there any real definite proof that Jesus and John, his favorite disciple, lived among the Essenes, and were strongly influenced by them?"

"It's puzzling to hear you say that the expressions *Son of Man* and *Messiah* have altogether different meanings in Hebrew, and I'd like further explanation, if you don't mind."

(Here, for the benefit of my present readers, I may say that the Semitic tongue, whether Hebrew or Aramaic, framed the expression *Son of Man* to mean *mankind,* in the English sense of the words, literally "man's child," or as in the German, *Menschenkind*; while the Hebrew term *Messiah* means *Anointed One.*)

"Why is it that many biblical scholars think that Jesus lived in India for a while, and studied with the priests there?"

"Am I correct in understanding that the First Enoch, out of which grew the Second, was written long before the birth of Christ, and what is the proof?"

(This question, I could see, aroused the curiosity and nodded doubt of most of the audience, as if it was a poser, indeed, until I described the famous Carbon 14 test, which scientifically determines the approximate age of the most ancient remains.)

"Will you please tell us the difference between the Pharisees, the Sadducees and the Essenes, and why the Essenes are never mentioned in the New Testament?"

"How much do the Dead Sea Scrolls prove the Higher Criticism right?"

All I could say to that was that the Higher Criticism and fresh translations of the Bible had illuminated many obscure corners of the sacred text, in word and act, which was all to the good, even though it might destroy fondly held ideas and imagery.

After all, the application and comparison of the contents of the Scrolls with the accepted tenets and forms of fundamental Christianity was just another important step in the right direction. The two Testaments must be judged as literature and history by exactly the same standards as used in studying nonbiblical literature, and not by arbitrary rules imposed by dogmatic liberals or conservatives. Looked at with philosophic impartiality, the Dead Sea Scrolls are helping to consolidate the historical unity of Old and New Testaments and futhering the continued vital search for the historic Jesus.

CHAPTER 13

Toward a New "Life" of Jesus

Now that the "Shrine of the Book" has been completed in Jerusalem to house the reconstituted Dead Sea Scrolls (appropriately, it is an underground, air-conditioned "cave" of man's making), it will be a destination of countless tourists and scholars from all parts of the world. Since their accidental discovery by a Bedouin goatherd, these Scrolls have been studied by savants, who have published their findings and various theories concerning their content. In 1957, a German bibliographer compiled a list of 1,538 titles of books on the subject, and the word *Qumranology* has been coined in Germany to denote the vast interest aroused in the Scrolls.

Theologians, of course, together with historians, philologists, paleographers and archaeologists have been drawn to these miraculously preserved manuscripts of two thousand years ago. Naturally, imaginative writers will find these sectarian documents of a long-vanished life a tempting source for fictional purposes. Imagine what novelists such as Sigrid Undset, Gustave Flaubert and Nikos

Kazantzakis could have done with such a subject (remember *Kristen Lavransdatter, Salammbo* and *The Last Temptation of Christ*). But contemporary novelists will be quick to meet the tremendous challenge of the Dead Sea Scrolls' story value. Dozens of provocative themes lie in wait for the inventive mind.

However, of all the " 'ologies" and " 'ists" involved in the serious riddle of Qumran and its caves, theology takes the lead because of the relationship between the Essenes, Jesus Christ and early Christianity. Bishop Lightfoot and his followers thought they had settled the question in the nineteenth century by dismissing the Essenes as having nothing to do with Christ and Christianity. A hundred years earlier, during the Age of Enlightenment, discussions frequently revolved around these questions: Was Jesus God? Was he or wasn't he an Essene? Wasn't Christianity the product of Essenism? Debates were long and hot and volumes (or pamphlets) pro and con were printed and distributed.

Illustrative of that rationalistic age is a sentence from a letter (dated October 17, 1770) written by Frederick the Great to encyclopedist d'Alembert: "Jesus was really an Essene; he was imbued with the Essene ethics, which, in their turn, owe much to Zeno [a Greek stoic philosopher]."

The New Testament had become the target of "advanced" thinking. France was in a turmoil of rationalism and England had been infected, but Germany was in the forefront with its "Lives" of Jesus Christ in "modernistic" vein. Between 1768 and 1816, the copious works of such esteemed scholars as Hess, Reinhard, Opitz, Jacobi and Herder sought to sift the truth under the supernatural declarations and contradictory facts found in the Gospels. Delve and deduce as they would, it was impossible to harmonize the mystic Fourth Gospel with the three Synoptics of Mark, Matthew and Luke. Nevertheless, these German exegetes were kind to the miracles, which were demolished in later "Lives" written from the middle of the nineteenth century on.

Meanwhile, taking the rational trail into fiction, they mixed biblical fact and story. Two writers—Karl Friedrich Bahrdt and Karl Heinrich Venturini—led the way; between them, they turned out thousands of pages for the delectation of readers who were intrigued by the thrilling possibilities in the Christology presented. Verity didn't matter. Excitement was all.

Of particular interest today is the use Bahrdt and Venturini made of the Essenes, who are presented as members of a powerful secret organization, penetrating all levels of society and bent on founding a new, glorious religion on a reformed Judaism. So they set their stage, and choose their cast of characters.

For their hero, they select a dreamy, idealistic young man who proves an innocent, willing tool in the Essene plot to manipulate the drama of Messiahship, the Crucifixion, the Resurrection and the Ascension. Every move is foreseen and worked out. Their enormous social and political power guarantees their hero-puppet against death. Jesus is not slain on the cross; instead, he is given anodynes and medicines (provided by Luke, the marvelous physician), and is rescued for the Resurrection and the Ascension, both of which have been carefully staged. Finally, Jesus is kidnaped by the Essenes and taken to an unknown place, where he becomes the head of the sect.

Melodramatic and childishly farfetched as the Bahrdt and Venturini stories were, they were in the "modern" vein of eighteenth-century thought and were eagerly received by the public. It is difficult today to accept the farfetched explanation that the two authors concoct. For instance, they explain the feeding of the five thousand with the five loaves of bread and two fishes by creating a stocked cave, out of which a concealed conspirator hands the food to Christ for distribution. In walking on the sea, Jesus glides over a submerged raft prepared as a prop. Healings were due to magical drugs, and the raising from the dead was simply the restoration of victims of coma.

Ridiculous as this may seem, the authors were not activated by any idea of fooling the readers or of making the Essenes villains. Rather, they were serious theological students, and sought to expose the "superstition" of the four Evangels. They represented the Essenes as benevolent villains whose connivery was designed to make the world a better place in which to live. The two writers were respected enough in their own time to inspire a school, a generation later, which carried on their imaginative mixtures of fact and fiction, and of which Richard von der Alm and Ludwig Roack were leading exponents.

Concurrently, the purely theological writers of "Lives" of Jesus went from rigid rationalism to a liberalism that was prelude to skepticism, the inevitable progress in this field of critical literature. All of these "Lives" had the same thing in common: they sought to present a "modernistic" Jesus, because the New Testament Jesus was too "improbable" for the enlightened people of the day. The proponents of the ideal wanted to find the historic Jesus beneath his alleged godhood.

Foremost among the nineteenth century liberals was David Friedrich Strauss, whose biography of Jesus Christ was issued and reissued in the period 1835-40, and almost immediately made him famous and infamous the world over. Seldom had a work of this kind produced such a storm of controversy in Germany, France, England and the United States. The "advanced" segment of his audience was delighted at his iconoclasm. What courage! What brilliant thinking! But average, intelligent citizens were outraged at his tasteless subversion of sacred Scripture. Such headings as "Sea Stories and Fish Stories" for a chapter on nature miracles aroused widespread ire and protest. Strauss, a modest scholar withal, went to the extreme of writing a new "Life" for the large offended public. This satisfied nobody, and the well-meaning man retired to obscurity.

Albert Schweitzer, in his classic *Quest of the Historical Jesus,* says, "It was a dead book, in spite of the many editions which it went through," but adds, "Strauss is no mere destroyer of untenable solutions, but also the prophet of a coming advance in knowledge."

La Vie de Jésus (The Life of Jesus), written in 1863 by Ernest Renan, was in the Strauss vein, and met with similar response from the international public. The opposition it stirred up was so indignant that the French government felt forced to remove Renan from the chair of Professor of Semitic Languages at the Collège de France, while the Pope put his book on the Index Expurgatorius. (Renan was a Catholic.)

Nevertheless, Renan continued to cast a spell of enchantment over readers with his rare literary charm. His prose witchery brought Jesus to life more vividly than had any preceding work of the kind. Indubitably, Renan was a skeptic at heart, though he consistently avoided giving any explanation of his nonsupport of miracles. Declaring himself a historian, not a theologian, his answer was always the same polite evasion: "We do not say miracle is impossible. We say only that there has never been a satisfactorily authenticated miracle."

Schweitzer, at the end of his long, well-documented *Quest,* concludes that neither learning nor imagination has succeeded in capturing the "historic" Jesus. With enormous scholarly patience and knowledge, he read and analyzed scores of "Lives," mostly German. Such a search, he intimates, was an *ignis fatuus*. He gave it up with this rather remarkable admission:

> "The ideal Life of Jesus at the close of the nineteenth century is the Life which Heinrich Julius Holtzmann did not write—but which can be pieced together from his commentary on the Synoptic Gospels and his New Testament theology. It is ideal because, for one thing, it is unwritten, and arises only in the idea of the reader by the aid of his own imagination, and, for another, because it is traced only in the most general outline . . . so that

anyone can carry out the construction in his own way."

Other highly esteemed scholarly critics agree with Schweitzer that it is impossible to find a "historic" Jesus, for the records are few and overlaid with supernatural emphasis. But Joseph Klausner, in his *Jesus of Nazareth* (1925), written for Jews in Hebrew, said:

"Following in Renan's footsteps came many writers of 'The Life of Jesus' from the liberal point of view. All the 'Lives' have the same thing in common: They seek to present to modern people a *modernist* Jesus, because the historic Jesus was too bizarre for the over-enlightened folk of today; he was too close to the Jewish ideas of the time of the Second Temple. . . . But the first decades of the twentieth century mark a noticeable change, not so much in the study of the Gospels as in the study of the character and teachings of Jesus and, especially, in the study of the Jewish environment."

Doesn't that illumine the vast possibilities of the Qumran Scrolls for new interpretations of that environment and its influence, and Jesus' possible association with the Essenes? Renan, a hundred years ago, said: "Christianity is an Essenism which has largely succeeded." And for our own particular gratification, he also declared that in the history of the origins of Christianity, the most important sources would be apocryphal works, such as the Book of Enoch and the Testaments of the Twelve Patriarchs, both of which have been considered of Essene authorship. "The Book of Enoch in particular," said the French savant, "was much read in Jesus' entourage. Some of the sayings ascribed to Jesus by the Synoptic Gospels are presented in the Epistle attributed to Saint Barnabas as being from Enoch."

What would Renan have made of his *Vie de Jésus* had the Dead Sea Scrolls appeared at the time he was planning his book in Gaza, where he sojourned for the atmosphere and color of the Holy Land? The Essenes would have offered him incomparable testimony. The Manual of Discipline, the Damascus Document, the Thanksgiving Hymns and the War of the Sons of Light Against the Sons of Darkness, would have provided wonderful new ideas for his book.

But the richness he missed has been gained by the scholars of today, whose years of devoted work on the Qumran Scrolls are already producing works of splendid enlightenment in various phases of the Essene mode of life and religious doctrines. Whether any of them will come closer to discovering the "historic" Jesus remains for the future to judge. At best, it will be a supremely arduous and dubious task to write such a "Life," not so much because of lack of credible source data, but because of the utter absence of knowledge of the chronological order of acts and sayings. Dr. Klausner is of the opinion that to find the "historic" Jesus requires the biographer, first of all, to forget Christian and Jewish dogma and to be as scientifically objective as is humanly possible. The human heart needs something more than the gloss provided by philologists, exegetical experts and erudite editors. This need has never been better expressed than by Giovanni Papini, whose *Life of Christ* electrified the world some forty years ago:

"The book we need is a living book, to make Christ more living, to set Christ the Ever-Living with loving vividness before the eyes of living men, to make us feel Him as actually and eternally present in our lives. We need a book which would show Him in all His living and present greatness— perennial and yet belonging to us moderns. . . . We need a book which would show in that tragic epic, written by both Heaven and Earth, the many teachings suited to us, suited to our time and life, which can be found there, not only in what Christ said, but in the very succession of events which begin in the stable at Bethlehem and end in a cloud over Bethany."

The labor required to fulfill this undertaking, so eloquently outlined by Papini, is nothing less than herculean. Equally difficult will be that of the novelist who sets out to re-create that troubled past with verisimilitude. It will call for the art found in *Quo Vadis?* and *The Last Days of Pompeii.*

There are many opportunities in the Qumran saga for the hand of the fiction writer. To begin with, there is the Essenes' heroic trek from the persecutions in Jerusalem into the bleak and barren Judean Desert, where they lived in caves and starved for their dissident beliefs. Think of the drama of the Teacher of Righteousness and his implacable foe, the "Wicked Priest"! Try to imagine the gigantic labor involved in building a refuge of rocks and in constructing a system to carry water over long distances. The close connection of John the Baptist with the Essene order provides still more food for imagination. And with the eventual admission of women to the community, what of the love interest? A novelist would find plenty there—the endless variations of the struggle between heart and mind, love and duty. And the fire-and-sword finale, when the Roman legion came and destroyed the then century-old community! Yes, Qumran has a wealth of story value awaiting the imaginative touch.

Already, one historical novelist has used the copper Qumran Scroll—the only metal one found—for an adventure tale. His tale is set in those tragic last days of the ascetic settlement; its protagonist is the man who engraved the extraordinary copper Scroll which describes the immense wealth of the Qumran Essenes—literally tons of gold—hidden in various places now no longer identifiable. It is estimated that the gold alone (there are tons of silver, also, and boxes of precious incense) would be worth about $200,000,000 at today's prices. But the official report of the copper Scroll's buried treasure dismisses any idea of hidden fortune, declaring it to be merely a list of traditions concerning where ancient wealth was supposedly secreted for one reason or another.

Immediately there arises a question: Why would the Essenes, whose first principle was poverty, have made such a timeproof record and where would they have gotten that enormous wealth?

"It is difficult," says the official report, "to understand why the Essenes of Qumran were so much concerned with these stories of hidden treasure, and especially why they saw fit to engrave them on copper, which at that time was a costly metal. It is also curious to learn that there was a second copy of this document giving explanations which we should very much like to know. . . ."

If that should turn up in future search of the caves, what a sequel there would be to a story already fantastic enough for an Arabian Nights tale!

CHAPTER 14

The Wrath to Come?

In 1961, C. P. Snow made a calm but appalling prediction: "Within at most ten years, some of these bombs are going off. I am saying this as responsibly as I can. That is a certainty. On the one side, therefore, we have a finite risk [in governmental agreements]. On the other side we have a certainty of disaster. Between a risk and a certainty, a sane man does not hesitate."

And in a speech given the same year, General Douglas MacArthur spoke of the store of nuclear weapons—enough to destroy five times over, every living man, woman and child on earth: "War in the Nuclear Age has lost its meaning. If you lose you are annihilated. If you win, you stand only to lose. . . . It contains now only the germs of double suicide."

Are we all, then, leaders and led, engaged in a "dance of death"—knowing we are, yet incapable of stopping? Sir Arthur Conan Doyle wrote a fantastic short story during World War I in which the world, in its spin around the sun, passes through a vast expanse of a gas that clings to it and sets mankind mad until its last vapors vanish. As everybody knows, Sir Arthur was a devotee of psychic phenomena, and this tale may have had its origin there.

However, one doesn't have to be psychic to speculate or to worry about the effects of the split atom on humanity and its dwelling place. Some curse science for its discovery. Others find philosophic comfort in such counsel as that given in Psalm 90: "Thou turnest man to destruction; and sayest, Return again, ye children of men. . . . So teach us to number our days, that we may apply our hearts unto wisdom."

There are a thousand different thoughts on the envisioned cataclysm, not all despairing or resigned. An accidentally overheard conversation between an old man and his middle-aged companion, went like this:

"What would you say is the reason for this travel craze going on today?" asked the younger man.

"People want to see the world before they lose it," smiled the old gentleman.

"How 'lose' it?" asked the vigorous paterfamilias.

"Don't tell me you haven't heard of the atom bomb, Dick!"

"Sure I have, and I've made a bet that it will be used before we get to the moon."

"So you're betting to lose!" chuckled the graybeard. "When are you going to collect if we all go up in smoke?"

"Oh, of course, I really hope to lose. By the way, have you heard that the real, deep-down reason for getting to the moon is to escape from the end of the world here?"

"Yes, and the reason people see flying saucers is the hope of rescue from outer space before our doomsday dawns. Is there anything sillier than that, Dick?"

"That's a laugh! I like the guy who said of the atomic stuff, that men had gotten hold of God's matchbox and didn't know what to do with it. Ever hear that one?"

Until the outbreak of World War I, men flattered themselves that they were learning to be better brothers, and pointed to the Peace Palace at The Hague, founded by Andrew Carnegie, as the symbol of the end to fratricide among nations. A brutal awakening came with the international murder of millions, to which was added the slaughter of as many more millions in World War II. Apocalyptically, Satan was let loose to deceive and devastate mankind.

Curiously pertinent to this dominant evil was the prophecy, nine hundred years ago, of St. Hildegard of Bingen, Germany, who foresaw the rise of Antichrist (the Devil). Her words could be interpreted to mean a power much like that of science today. In all probability, her vision was inspired by the passage often applied to the present era, "until the times of the Gentiles be fulfilled" (Luke 21:24).

St. Malachy, born in Armagh, Ireland, in 1094, prophesied on all the popes to the end of the papacy, with startling accuracy. What he said of the last pope before the climactic holocaust set for A.D. 2000 brings to mind the late Pope John XXIII. The final Holy Father was to be the *Pastor Angelicus* of tradition, who would achieve the unity of faiths preparatory to Christ's Second Coming.

Evidently, the date for the "end of days" is thus set for the close of the twentieth century, which current fictionists have adopted for their "democracy of death." Saint and seer seem to have given them their clue.

Consistent with this imaginative mood, let us review briefly the provocative course of prophecy of the "end of days," from the Day of Yahweh to the Book of Revelation, thence through the intervening centuries to the present hour of fear and hope, during which the state of mind might be compared to that of the Jews during the tumultuous period we are weighing.

We have touched on the Old and New Testament eschatological expectations and pseudepigraphic previsions, the Books of Daniel and Revelation being supreme examples. Powerful, too, is the description of the final apocalypse given by Jesus in Mark 13 and Luke 21. Many biblical exegetes have declared these to be interpolations, not in keeping with the spirit of Christ as exemplified throughout the Gospels. I am inclined to agree with this criticism, judging from the treatment of the Last Judgment in The Secrets of Enoch which, unlike that in First Enoch, dwells on rewards to the righteous rather than on punishments for the wicked. Obviously, such theorizing makes little difference to the average Christian of today, whose whole interest in eschatology is centered on a man-made one in thermonuclear warfare.

Taking their cue from the Bible as to the "times of the Gentiles" for the "end of days," the majority of prophecies bearing on the cosmic cataclysm during the last thousand years have been announced through the media of astrology, clairvoyance, dream-trance and so-called "second sight." Repeated failure of their predictions has not deterred the prophets in the least. New ones arise with each generation. Even in this most materialistic epoch of ours, there are God-fearing cults that look upon the atomic bomb as a chosen instrument of the Divine to usher in the Second Coming.

This same world-ending event was announced for the year A.D. 999 by influential millenarian leaders, who believed that the thousand-year period of grace before the Second Coming of Christ was drawing to an end. The credulous public of the Middle Ages was swept into fanatical action. Lords, knights and serfs sold their worldly possessions, gathered their wives and children together, and headed for Jerusalem, where the Son of God was scheduled to appear for the Last Judgment. Naturally, many of the pilgrims starved and died on the long journey, but the survivors pressed on, singing hymns, chanting psalms and saying prayers, their eyes searching for signs and omens in the sky. How many reached Jerusalem is not recorded, but we do know that the expected phenomenon did not take place.

However, the fiasco was forgotten with time, and in the sixteenth century two famous seers came to the fore —Nostradamus, who is credited with genuine predictive powers, and Mother Shipton, the more or less legendary

Englishwoman who was celebrated for her prophetic verses. (She is said to have "seen" the modern realization of the automobile, telegraph, radio, aircraft, steamship and submarine.) But the beldame failed in picking an earthly curtain time:

> "The world to an end shall come
> In eighteen hundred and eighty-one."

In contrast to this humiliating error, Nostradamus, the far-seeing Frenchman, envisioned only a devastating attack "from the sky" in October, 1999, on the eve of the second millennium, but the "end of days" wasn't due until A.D. 3429. That may give some welcome respite to those who are dreading megaton-bomb annihilation.

The nineteenth and twentieth centuries have also produced prophesiers of the date of the "end of days." The last century brought the once-famed William Miller, an American who founded a sect named after himself. Like his predecessors of the A.D. 999 hoax, Miller calculated his end-all date from biblical mathematics, particularly those obscure calculations in Daniel (8:14). Christ will return on March 21, 1843, or March 21, 1844, Miller told his followers, who prepared their ascension robes in readiness for their translation into heaven. Twice the faithful gathered for the glorious meeting, and twice nothing happened. "The world is reeling to and fro like a drunkard," the leader assured the Millerites, but all that appeared in the sky were ominous rings around the sun and the awesome tail of the great comet of 1843, measuring 108,000,000 miles in length.

Sorrowfully, after this double fiasco, the only world to end was Miller's. Thousands of his followers deserted him. A broken man, he died alone in his Vermont home, discredited and beaten by his own honest delusion.

Among modern prophets, it is fitting to include Tolstoy, Spengler and H. G. Wells, who forecast the future without any pretense of psychic power but with common sense and penetrating intellect. None of these three sages, with the possible exception of Tolstoy, gave the western world much chance of survival. Nuclear annihilation didn't enter their prognostications; evidence was all around that the well-known lethal acids of materialism, amorality and Mammon were hastening the process of self-destruction.

Tolstoy was undoubtedly head and shoulders above the other two. The vision he is said to have had shortly before his death in 1910 has been reported by his daughter, Anastasia:

> "This is a revelation of events of a universal character, which must shortly come to pass. Their spiritual outlines are now before my eyes. I see floating upon the sea of human fate the huge silhouette of a nude woman. She is—with her beauty, her poise, her smile, her jewels—a super-Venus. Nations rush madly after her, each of them eager to attract her especially. But she, like an eternal courtesan, flirts with all. In her hair—an ornament of diamonds and rubies—is engraved her name: Commercialism. As alluring and bewitching as she seems, much destruction and agony follow in her wake. . . ."

Then, after a pause, the dying genius continued his revelation in the vein of an ancient prophet. The vision would seem to have depicted World War I and its aftermath:

> "I see all Europe in flames. I hear the lamentations on huge battlefields. . . . The world will form a federation of the United States of nations. . . . There will remain only four great giants—the Anglo-Saxons, the Latins, the Slavs and the Mongolians. . . . The ethical idea has almost vanished. Humanity is without moral feeling. . . . The antinational wars in Europe, the class war in America and the race

wars in Asia have strangled progress for half a century."

Tolstoy's super-Venus suited Spengler and Wells in their thinking. Like another John the Baptist, Spengler proclaimed his controversial doctrine: "The end is at hand. The downfall of the Occident is approaching. Western Europe has passed its zenith and it must now look forward to a rapid decline . . . [and] range itself with the extinct civilizations."

On the other hand, when Oswald Spengler was still in short pants, the Russian Theosophist and occultist, Madame Blavatsky (1831-91), said that the Mahatmas, whose disciple she was, foresaw a race, beginning in 1975 among the western nations, that would be "grander, nobler and more spiritual" than their history had yet recorded. Incidentally, before her death, the mystic lady predicted the imminent discovery of a new tremendous power. (The X ray was discovered in 1895, which made possible the development of the atom.)

"It is a vibratory force," said Madame Blavatsky, "which when aimed at an army of 100,000 men will reduce it to ashes, as it would a dead rat!"

"Crazy!" said the non-Theosophist world.

"Was she?" we ask now in the face of nuclear power.

Whatever may be the true explanation of psychic phenomena, the determinism of God's Will and the freedom of man's will has always been the great antinomy of Hebrew-Christian thought; the ability to fix the date of the "end of days" has proved to be beyond human powers of calculation or prediction. Even Christ himself said, "Of that day and that hour knoweth no man, no, not the angels which are in heaven, neither the Son, but the Father" (Mark 13:32).

But what about the very real eschatological threat looming over us now? Has the Creator given His children the right to destroy all life at a blow—a life which has taken billions of years to fashion? Is this to be ordained as the Last Judgment—that man is free to choose his eternal fate?

"God's dice are always loaded," warns Emerson.

Besides the concrete answer of technology to the awful problem of its doomsday machines poised to obliterate mankind, psychology has a word to say that, unfortunately, solves nothing, but presents an opposite reaction to the threat of human extinction. In his old age, Sigmund Freud wrote two books, entitled *Beyond the Pleasure Principle* and *Civilization and Its Discontents.* Characteristically, the father of the Oedipus complex dwells on the primal struggle in the human aspects between Eros (the life principle) and Death (self-destruction). He describes this struggle as "the hostility of each one against all, and of all against each one." Metapsychologically expressed: "The purpose of all life is death."

Carl Gustav Jung, in *Psyche and Symbol,* disagrees: "The instinct to survive is aroused as a reaction against the tendency to mass suicide represented by the H-bomb, and the underlying political schism of the world."

Both of these renowned psychologists have now gone to the place where the answer, if any, lies.

General Omar Bradley, a practical philosopher, put in a nontheoretical oar: "We have too many men of science; too few men of God. We have grasped the mystery of the atom and rejected the Sermon on the Mount. Man is stumbling blindly through a spiritual darkness while toying with the precarious secrets of life and death. The world has achieved brilliance without wisdom, power without conscience. Ours is a world of nuclear giants and ethical infants."

The author of The Secrets of Enoch, a supreme lover of mankind, held a vision of the "end of days" that dwelt more on reward than punishment. In this he differed from his predecessor, the author of First Enoch, whose apocalyptic description of the Last Judgment missed no item of horror and terror, although praising God's goodness and equity. The merciful writer of The Secrets of Enoch modified this frightful emphasis. He did not fail to mention hell fire, but he stressed the happier issue: "When all the creation which the Lord has made shall end, Blessed are the righteous who shall escape at the Lord's Great Judgment, for their countenance shall shine like the sun . . ." (65:6).

Shalom!

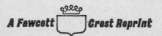